A Companion to Literary Forms

A Companion to Literary Forms

Padmaja Ashok

Orient BlackSwan

A COMPANION TO LITERARY FORMS

ORIENT BLACKSWAN PRIVATE LIMITED

Registered Office
3-6-752 Himayatnagar, Hyderabad 500 029, Telangana, India
Email: centraloffice@orientblackswan.com

Other Offices
Bengaluru, Chennai, Guwahati, Hyderabad, Kolkata,
Mumbai, New Delhi, Noida, Patna, Visakhapatnam

First Published 2015
Reprinted 2016, 2017, 2019, 2020, 2022, 2023

ISBN 978 81 250 5865 6

036348

Typeset in Life BT 11/14 *by*
Orient BlackSwan

Printed at
Yash Printographics, Noida

Published by
Orient Blackswan Private Limited
3-6-752 Himayatnagar, Hyderabad 500 029, Telangana, India
Email: info@orientblackswan.com

Contents

Preface

Literature may be defined as the best thoughts of an author, presented in the best manner. From this description of literature, one can easily understand that it is made up of two parts—content and form. When asked to talk about literature, one often immediately enumerates its various forms, such as poetry, drama, fiction and nonfiction. It is clear that the forms in which literature finds its expression are as important as the content that they convey. It is therefore essential for a student of literature to have a thorough knowledge of the various forms of literature in order to enhance his/her appreciation of the subject.

The study of literary forms is a highly interesting one, as one gets to learn how human thought gradually evolved. It is fascinating to trace the incredible journey of literature from its crude, early beginnings, when songs and stories were passed on from one generation to another orally, to the sophisticated, complex and erudite works of contemporary authors.

A study of literary genres and forms plays a key role in sensitising the student of literature to the nuances of a work of art. For example, when we learn about the absence of the drop curtain in the Elizabethan stage, we begin to notice the unique manner in which each scene is concluded and how the characters exit the stage. We then understand the practical reason why, at the end of Shakespeare's play *Hamlet*, Horatio gives detailed instructions to take away the dead bodies of Hamlet and the others. Our attention is also drawn towards the rhyming couplet at the end of each scene. All these features were a direct consequence of the absence of the drop curtain! To give another example, learning about the features and conventions of an epic would definitely enhance our understanding and appreciation of Milton's great work,

Paradise Lost. No course in literature can be complete without an adequate knowledge of literary forms.

This book is designed to cater to the needs of the students of English literature. Each form is first defined in a simple manner; its features are then listed, and suitable examples are given. In addition to examining the chief forms, the book discusses the innovations undergone by each, and also looks at various trends in literary criticism.

A Companion to Literary Forms is the result of more than two decades of teaching literary forms by the author. It will prove to be a useful guide to not only undergraduate students, but also to postgraduate students and research scholars as a ready reckoner of several useful terms. It is sincerely hoped that both students and teachers will find the book a helpful companion in their study of literary forms.

1

Poetry

Poetry is one of the earliest literary forms to have evolved. It has its origins in prehistoric times, when people made use of poetic language, singing to the accompaniment of musical instruments. Thus, poetry existed in the oral form long before the invention of writing. The ancient Sumerian poem *Epic of Gilgamesh* is one of the earliest poems in existence. It is said to have been composed around 1800BCE. The ancient Indian *Vedas*, dating back to about 1700–1100BCE, are another example of early literature. These texts were passed down orally, from one generation to another, till the gradual development of writing.

As a form of art, poetry has evolved through the centuries, spawning many literary forms in cultures around the world. Poetry has adapted itself to the rapid developments in both language and technology, and continues to be a major form of human artistic expression.

How may one define poetry? British author William Henry Hudson said that poetry is 'an interpretation of life through imagination and feeling'. Thomas Carlyle believed that poetry was 'musical thought', while Edgar Allan Poe called it 'the rhythmic creation of beauty'. The word is derived from the ancient Greek word *ποιητής* ('poiētēs') meaning 'creator'. A poet is therefore a creator, who, through his imagination, interprets life and arouses feelings of delight, sorrow, amusement or introspection in the reader. The ultimate aim of poetry is to give pleasure.

Poetry is distinct from prose in that it is literature in metrical form. The presence of **metre**, **rhythm** and **rhyme** distinguishes poetry from prose. Some critics have questioned the necessity of metre and rhyme for poetry, and indeed there do exist very good poems that do not have metre and rhyme. However, it is the sound and rhythm of poetry that first attracts people to a poem. The use of metre lifts us from the ordinary world of everyday experience. Rhyme and metre contribute greatly to the aesthetic pleasure that we derive from poetry. Further, when words are arranged in a certain rhythmical order, they gain new meaning and power, and appeal to our emotions in a magical way. The presence of rhythm, rhyme and metre played an important part in preserving ancient poetry, since these techniques helped our ancestors to remember the lines better, and thus allowed them to pass their poetry down the centuries before it could be written down.

Poetry (and art in general) differs from subjects like science in its treatment of truth. While the poet and the scientist may both deal with nature, their approaches are different. The poet awakens a sense of wonder at the mystery of the world around us; the scientist tries to explain the mystery to us. While science (and its related fields) concerns itself with factual accuracy and literal truth, poetry often uses the imagination to transcend reality. This does not mean that poetry perpetuates lies. The truth that the poet presents to the world is called '**poetic truth**'. The poet's feelings are genuine and sincere, and he looks beyond the surface level of truth (such as scientific or historical fact) in order to reveal important patterns and connections, and thus to interpret life.

The poet enjoys what is called '**poetic licence**'. In its most narrow sense, it is the freedom taken by a poet to bend the conventions of diction. It is the liberty given to poets to manipulate language, distort syntax and use archaisms to suit his needs. Gerard Manley Hopkins, for example, makes use of several archaic dialect words in his poems and also coins words of his own, such as 'twinsles', which is a combination of 'twines' and 'dwindles'. He also creates compound adjectives with a hyphen—'dapple-dawn-drawn Falcon'—or sometimes without a hyphen—'rolling level underneath him steady air'. In a broader sense, poetic licence is the freedom given to all artists to violate the literal truth in order to present poetic truth. The poet may change historical fact (Shakespeare did it frequently in his history plays), use anachronisms (see page 117), or ask his readers for a willing suspension of disbelief. However, such distortions of fact do not reduce our enjoyment of the work of art. Indeed, poetic licence is often employed to enhance either the aesthetic beauty or the poetic truth of a work of art.

Classification of poetry

The vast body of poetry may be classified under two broad headings for the sake of convenience—objective and subjective. In **objective poetry**, the poet is detached from what he is writing. He describes, in an impersonal manner, the actions and passions of other people with little reference to his own self and personal feelings. **Subjective poetry**, on the other hand, is a reflection of the poet's own personal feelings and experiences.

Objective poetry is much older than subjective poetry. It is believed to have originated among the primitive people of prehistoric times, when mankind had not yet learnt to read and write. These people were more interested in the physical world around them, and in the deeds and objects that were a part of their lives. There was little room for deep thinking, emotions and feelings. Poetry, as it existed then, was more of a communal affair than a personal one.

Subjective poetry came into existence much later, when people began to give importance to their thoughts, feelings and emotions, and to the growing need to share them.

This broad categorisation is useful when one wishes to study the different forms of poetry. However, it cannot be followed strictly as there is often an overlapping of the two.

Objective poetry	Subjective poetry
Ballad	Lyric
Epic	Ode
Metrical romance	Elegy
Dramatic monologue	Idyll
Limerick	Sonnet
	Epistle

Ballad

A ballad may be defined as a song that narrates a story. The word 'ballad' is derived from the Latin *ballare* which means 'to dance'. Ballads could be said to have been in existence thousands of years ago when people had still not learnt to read or write. They were songs sung by wandering minstrels to the accompaniment of musical instruments and dance. Often one person sang, while the others danced and joined in on the refrain.

Features of a ballad

- A ballad often narrates stories of love, adventure, war and bravery. The theme may be tragic or comic. Often, there is a touch of the supernatural. Basic emotions, such as love, hatred and pity, are prominently dealt with in ballads.
- A ballad usually deals with a single episode. The story is told through both dialogue and action.
- The language used is very simple as the poet wished to be understood easily by all his listeners.
- The ballad often begins abruptly. Sometimes an unknown person asks a question and the answer forms the rest of the ballad.
- For example, these are the opening lines of the Scottish ballad 'The Demon Lover'—

> Oh, where have you been, long, long love,
> This seven years and more?
> Oh, I've come to seek my former vows
> Ye granted me before.

- A ballad has stock epithets such as 'blood-red wine' and 'merry men'.
- A characteristic feature of ballads is repetition, usually in the form of **refrains**—lines that are repeated at intervals in a poem or a song, especially at the end of a stanza. The word 'refrain' originated from the Old French word *refraindre*, which means 'to repeat'. An example of a refrain is the line 'Sweet Thames, run softly, till I end my song' which ends every stanza of Edmund Spenser's *Prothalamion*. The refrain may be in the form of a phrase or even a single word; for example, the repetition of the words 'Nevermore' in Edgar Allan Poe's poem, 'The Raven'.
- The ballad verse consists of a quatrain with alternating iambic tetrameter (four foot) and trimeter (three foot) lines. The rhyme scheme is usually ABCB or ABAB. The following lines are from the Scottish ballad 'The Wife of Usher's Well'—

> There lived | a wife | at Ush | er's well, a
> And a weal | thy wife | was she; b
> She had | three stout | and stal | wart sons, c
> And sent | them o'er | the sea. b

POPULAR BALLAD, FOLK BALLAD

This type of ballad, also known as the **traditional ballad**, is anonymous and is passed on from generation to generation by word of mouth. It belongs to the oral tradition and is still in existence among the illiterate people of northern Greece, Sicily and the Balkans. Since these ballads were never written, each singer who learnt the ballad introduced his own changes. The popular ballad therefore exists in many forms.

British ballads have been collected by several people since the eighteenth century. The most well-known of these anthologies is Francis J. Child's *English and Scottish Popular Ballads* (1882–98), which contains 305 ballads, including 'Sir Patrick Spens', 'Clerk Saunders', 'The Twa Corbies' and 'The Ballad of Chevy Chase'.

The stories and legends of the twelfth-century English outlaw Robin Hood, who robbed the rich to help the poor, inspired several ballads that are known as the '**Robin Hood ballads**'. Child collected about thirty-eight ballads in which Robin Hood was featured. These ballads are believed to have been composed over hundreds of years. Robin Hood Ballads are known for their merry nature and belong to the popular or folk tradition.

BROADSIDE BALLAD

This type of a ballad is printed on one side of a single sheet of poor quality paper. These were sold in bulk on the streets from the sixteenth century onwards by wandering peddlers. Most broadsides are sentimental in subject matter, containing stories of murder, execution or adventure. Public events were often published in broadsides and printers earned a lot of money through them. Only the growth of the newspaper put an end to the broadside.

LITERARY BALLAD

Literary or **lyrical ballads** are narrative poems written by poets in deliberate imitation of the form of the traditional ballad. These were particularly popular in the late eighteenth century, during the Romantic period. The Scottish literary giants Robert Burns and Sir Walter Scott collected and wrote their own ballads, using the form to create an artistic product. In England, William Wordsworth and Samuel Taylor Coleridge produced a collection titled *Lyrical Ballads* (1798), which included Coleridge's 'The Rime of the Ancient Mariner'. John Keats's 'La Belle Dame sans Merci' (1819) is another example of the literary ballad.

MOCK BALLAD

This form mocks the seriousness of the literary ballad, and the theme is comic rather than tragic. It has all the features of a literary ballad, but everything is given a humorous twist. Excellent examples of mock ballads are William Maginn's 'The Rime of the Ancient Waggoner' and William Cowper's 'The Diverting History of John Gilpin' (1782).

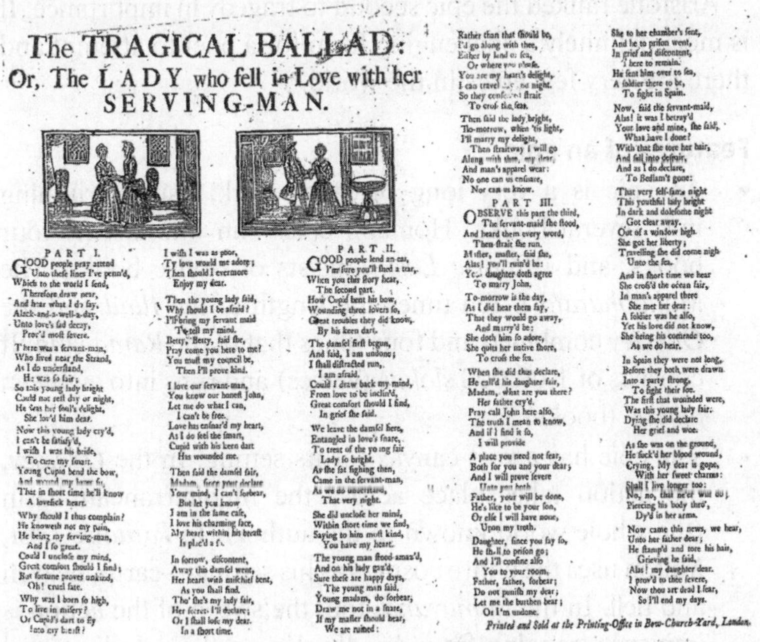

The TRAGICAL BALLAD:
Or, The LADY who fell in Love with her SERVING-MAN.

PART I.

GOOD people pray attend
Unto theſe lines I've penn'd,
Which to the world I ſend,
Therefore draw near,
And hear what I do ſay,
Alack-and-a-well-a-day,
Unto love's ſad decay,
Prov'd moſt ſevere.

There was a ſervant-man,
Who lived near the Strand,
As I do underſtand,
He was ſo fair;
So this young lady bright
Could not reſt day or night,
He was her ſoul's delight,
She lov'd him dear.

Now this young lady cry'd,
I can't be ſatiſfy'd,
I wiſh I was his bride,
To cure my ſmart.
Young Cupid bend the bow,
And wound my lover ſo,
That in ſhort time he'll know
A loveſick heart.

Why ſhould I thus complain?
He knoweth not my pain,
He being my ſerving-man,
And I ſo great.
Could I uncloſe my mind,
Great comfort ſhould I find;
But fortune proves unkind,
Oh! cruel fate.

Why was I born ſo high,
To live in miſery?
Or Cupid's dart to fly
Into my breaſt!

I wiſh I was as poor,
Ty love would me adore;
Then ſhould I evermore
Enjoy my dear.

Then the young lady ſaid,
Why ſhould I be afraid?
I'll bring my ſervant maid
To tell my mind.
Betty, Betty, ſaid ſhe,
Pray come you here to me?
You muſt my council be,
Then I'll prove kind.

I love our ſervant-man,
You know our honeſt John,
Let me do what I can,
I can't be free.
Love has enſnar'd my heart,
As I do feel the ſmart,
Cupid with his keen dart
Has wounded me.

Then ſaid the damſel fair,
Madam, ſince you declare
Your mind, I can't forbear,
But let you know
I am in the ſame caſe,
I love his charming face,
My heart within his breaſt
Is plac'd a ſo.

In ſorrow, diſcontent,
Away this damſel went,
Her heart with miſchief bent,
As you ſhall find.
Tho' ſhe's my lady fair,
Her ſecrets I'll declare;
Or I ſhall loſe my dear.
In a ſhort time.

PART II.

GOOD people lend an ear,
I'm ſure you'll ſhed a tear,
When you this ſtory hear,
The ſecond part.
How Cupid bent his bow,
Wounding three lovers ſo,
Great troubles they did know,
By his keen dart.

The damſel firſt begun,
And ſaid, I am undone;
I ſhall diſtracted run,
I am afraid.
Could I draw back my mind,
From love to be inclin'd,
Great comfort ſhould I find,
In grief ſhe ſaid.

We leave the damſel here,
Entangled in love's ſnare,
To treat of the young fair
Lady ſo bright.
As ſhe ſat ſighing then,
Came in the ſervant-man,
As we do underſtand,
That very night.

She did uncloſe her mind,
Within ſhort time we find,
Saying to him moſt kind,
You have my heart.

The young man ſtood amaz'd,
And on his lady gaz'd,
Sure theſe are happy days,
The young man ſaid.
Young madam, do forbear,
Draw me not in a ſnare,
If my maſter ſhould hear,
We are ruined:

Rather than that ſhould be,
I'd go along with thee,
Either by land or ſea,
Or where you pleaſe.
You are my heart's delight,
I can travel day and night.
So they conferr'd ſtrait
To croſs the ſeas.

Then ſaid the lady bright,
To-morrow, when 'tis light,
I'll marry my delight,
Then ſtraitway I will go
Along with thee, my dear,
And man's apparel wear:
No one can us enſnare,
Nor can us know.

PART III.

OBSERVE this part the third,
The ſervant-maid ſhe ſtood,
And heard them every word,
Then ſtrait ſhe run.
Maſter, maſter, ſaid ſhe,
Alas! you'll ruin'd be:
Your daughter doth agree
To marry John.

To-morrow is the day,
As I did hear them ſay,
That they would go away,
And marry'd be:
She doth him ſo adore,
She quits her native ſhore,
To croſs the ſea.

When ſhe did thus declare,
He call'd his daughter fair,
Madam, what are you there?
Her father cry'd.
Pray call John here alſo,
The truth I mean to know,
And if I find it ſo,
I will provide

A place you need not fear,
Both for you and your dear;
And I will prove ſevere
Unto you both.
Father, your will be done,
He's like to be your ſon,
Or elſe I will have none,
Upon my troth.

Daughter, ſince you ſay ſo,
He ſhall to priſon go;
And I'll confine alſo
You to your room.
Father, father, forbear;
Do not puniſh my dear;
Let me the burthen bear;
Or I'm undone.

She to her chamber's ſent,
And he to priſon went,
In grief and diſcontent,
There to remain.
He ſent him over to ſea,
A ſoldier there to be,
To fight in Spain.

Now, ſaid the ſervant-maid,
Alas! it was I betray'd
Your love and mine, ſhe ſaid,
What have I done?
With that ſhe tore her hair,
And fell into deſpair,
And as I do declare,
To Bedlam's gone:

That very ſelf-ſame night
This youthful lady bright
In dark and doleſome night
Got clear away.
Out of a window high
She got her liberty;
Travelling ſhe did come nigh
Unto the ſea.

And in ſhort time we hear
She croſs'd the ocean fair,
In man's apparel there
She met her dear:
A ſoldier was he alſo,
Yet his love did not know,
She being his comrade too,
As we do hear.

In Spain they were not long,
Before they both were drawn
Into a party ſtrong,
To fight their foe.
The firſt that wounded were,
Was this young lady fair.
Dying ſhe did declare
Her grief and woe.

As ſhe was on the ground,
He ſuck'd her blood wound,
Crying, My dear is gone,
With her ſweet charms:
Shall I live longer too:
No, no, that ne'er will do;
Piercing his body thro',
Dy'd in her arms.

Now came this news, we hear,
Unto her father dear;
He ſtamp'd and tore his hair,
Grieving he ſaid,
Alas! my daughter dear.
I prov'd to thee ſevere,
Now thou art dead I fear,
So I'll end my days.

Printed and Sold at the Printing-Office in Bow-Church-Yard, London.

IMAGE A: An eighteenth-century broadside ballad

Epic

An epic is a long narrative poem on the exploits of great heroes, told in a grand and elevated style. **Traditional** or **primary epics** combine myth, legend, folk tales and history, and are thus part of a nation's cultural history. These developed from an oral tradition. Important examples of such epics are Homer's *Iliad* and *Odyssey* (both composed circa eighth century BCE), the Indian *Ramayana* (attributed to Valmiki, circa fifth century BCE) and *Mahabharata* (attributed to Vyasa, circa fourth century BCE), and the Anglo-Saxon epic *Beowulf* (circa eighth century CE). **Literary** or **secondary epics** were written by poets who imitated the traditional form. To this category belong Virgil's *Aeneid* (first century BCE) and John Milton's *Paradise Lost* (1667).

Aristotle ranked the epic second to tragedy in importance. It is most definitely a challenging form for a poet to attempt and there are very few epics in the world.

Features of an epic

- An epic is a very long piece of work, usually running into several books. Homer's epics run into twenty-four books, and *Paradise Lost* consists of twelve books. The *Mahabharata* is ten times the length of the *Iliad* and the *Odyssey* combined and four times that of the *Ramayana*. It consists of 1,00,000 *slokas* (verses) and runs into eighteen *parvas* (books).
- The epic has a vast canvas for its setting. In the *Odyssey*, the action takes place across the Mediterranean basin (the whole world known to the author). In *Paradise Lost*, Milton uses the entire cosmos as his setting—earth, heaven and hell. In the *Ramayana*, too, the sweep of the action is immense, ranging from Ayodhya in northern India to Sri Lanka.

- The action depicted in an epic is also on a gigantic scale, often involving supernatural deeds and perilous journeys. The adventures of Achilles and Odysseus, and the latter's long journey back to his home; the mighty war in heaven and Satan's journey to the newly created world; the wanderings of the banished Pandavas and the terrible war at Kurukshetra; and Rama's quest across the country for Sita and his war against the forces of Ravana, are all examples of the magnificent scale of action in an epic.
- The time of action in an epic is also on a large scale. In Homer's epics, the action covers a period of more than ten years. In the Indian epics, too, the period of time is long. In *Paradise Lost*, the story ranges from before the creation of the universe to the end of the world.
- The epic is centred on a hero who is of great importance. In the *Iliad*, Achilles is the greatest of Greek warriors; in Milton's *Paradise Lost*, Adam is the first man and is a representative of the entire human race; and in the *Mahabharata*, the Pandavas are superhuman heroes who fight alongside gods.
- An epic shows gods and other supernatural beings taking part in the action. Homer makes use of the Olympian gods in his epics, while archangels, Christ and Satan appear in *Paradise Lost*. In the Indian epics, Krishna and Rama are the incarnations of Vishnu. Such actions of deities and supernatural beings were called the '**machinery**' in the eighteenth century.
- The language used in an epic is always elevated and formal to suit the grandeur of the theme. Milton uses Latinate diction and complex syntax to narrate the story of the fall of man. The grand style of epic poetry includes the usage of several classical allusions and epic similes. An **epic simile** is a long simile, running into more than twenty lines at times, in which the poet makes a detailed

comparison. This was first used by Homer in his epics to enhance the ceremonial quality of the narration. Hence they are also known as **Homeric similes**. The following is an example of an epic simile from *Paradise Lost*, Book IV. Here, Milton compares the Garden of Eden to several mythological gardens.

Not that fair field
Of Enna, where Proserpin gathering flowers,
Herself a fairer flower, by gloomy Dis
Was gathered—which cost Ceres all that pain
To seek her through the world—nor that sweet grove
Of Daphne, by Orontes and the inspired
Castalian spring, might with this Paradise
Of Eden strive; nor that Nyseian isle,
Girt with the river Triton, where old Cham,
Whom Gentiles Ammon call and Libyan Jove,
Hid Amalthea, and her florid son,
Young Bacchus, from his stepdame Rhea's eye;
Nor, where Abassin kings their issue guard,
Mount Amara (though this by some supposed
True Paradise) under the Ethiop line
By Nilus' head, enclosed with shining rock,
A whole day's journey high, but wide remote
From this Assyrian garden, where the Fiend
Saw undelighted all delight, all kind
Of living creatures, new to sight and strange.

Epic conventions

The writers of epics often imitated Homer to the extent that certain narrative elements have become conventions. These include the following—

- The poet begins the work with a **proposition** followed by an **invocation** to a muse. In the proposition, the author states his purpose, or his theme or 'argument'. In the invocation, the poet appeals to the muse for inspiration.

The following lines from Milton's *Paradise Lost* suitably illustrate both the proposition and the invocation.

> Of Man's first disobedience, and the fruit
> Of that forbidden tree whose mortal taste
> Brought death into the World, and all our woe,
> With loss of Eden, till one greater Man
> Restore us, and regain the blissful Seat,
> Sing, Heavenly Muse,...

- The narration in an epic typically begins **in medias res**, that is 'in the middle of the things'. *Paradise Lost* begins in Hell with Satan gathering forces and trying to organise his revenge. It is only after Book V that we learn about the war in Heaven which led to the banishment of Satan to Hell.
- Another important epic convention is the cataloguing of important characters. Milton gives a detailed description of the fallen angels in Book I of his epic. These characters are given set speeches to suit their particular character.
- In an epic, the characters are depicted playing some games. The game of dice in the *Mahabharata* is a very well-known example of this convention. In *Paradise Lost*, the fallen angels indulge in competitive games to while away the time till Satan returned from his visit to Paradise.

Mock-epic

A **mock-epic** or a **mock-heroic poem** is a parody of the serious epic. It has all the features and conventions of a serious epic but the intention is comic and usually satirical. The classical example of a mock-epic is the *Battle of the Frogs and Mice* (circa seventh century BCE), which is a parody of the Greek epic *Iliad*. Alexander Pope's *The Rape of the Lock* (1712) is an excellent example of a mock-epic in English.

Pope's poem narrates the incident of the cutting off of a lock of hair from a girl's head by an infatuated lover. The trivial incident is treated in an epic manner which gives rise to great humour. As a master of the classics, Pope was very familiar with epic conventions and features, and he included each and every aspect of the epic in his poem. The result is hilarious and delightful. The work has an invocation, a proposition, supernatural machinery, long speeches, epic similes, and the depiction of epic journeys, games and battles.

Metrical Romance

The metrical romance is another form of narrative poetry that resembles the epic. This genre includes verse stories told in the **Romance languages** (languages that descended from Latin, such as Spanish, Portuguese, French, Italian, Romanian and Catalan) which dealt with chivalry, knight-errantry, fighting, adventure, magic, and love. Later, the genre began to include similar stories written in English too. This form was popular from the Middle Ages to the nineteenth century.

Geoffrey Chaucer's 'The Knight's Tale' (from *The Canterbury Tales*, late fourteenth century), Ludovico Ariosto's *Orlando Furioso* (1532), Edmund Spenser's *The Faerie Queene* (1590–96), Walter Scott's 'The Lay of the Last Minstrel' (1805) and 'The Lady of the Lake' (1810) and Alfred Tennyson's *Idylls of the King* (1859–85) could be called metrical romances.

Dramatic Monologue

A dramatic monologue is the name given to a particular type of poem in which a single person, who is not the poet, narrates his experiences or shares his inner-most feelings. It is an objective poetic analysis of a subjective point of view. It was most popular during the Victorian era and Robert Browning was its chief exponent.

In such a poem, the speaker reveals his character through his monologue. It is not to be confused with the **soliloquy** of drama. In a soliloquy, a character gives voice to his inner thoughts and feelings. It is a device used by the dramatist in order to make the audience understand a complex character like Hamlet or Iago. The soliloquy is not meant to be heard by the other characters in the play. In a dramatic monologue, the speaker addresses one or more auditors whose presence is indicated to us through the poem.

Features of a dramatic monologue

- A dramatic monologue has all the elements of drama such as plot, character, dialogue and setting. Yet, it is a form of poetry and not drama as it is meant to be read and not performed on stage.
- A single person—who is not the poet—utters the whole poem.
- The speech is uttered by the speaker at some critical moment. For example, in Browning's 'Fra Lippo Lippi' (1855), the truant monk is caught by a watchman and the monologue is the monk's explanation. The Duke in Browning's 'My Last Duchess' (1842) is negotiating with an emissary for another bride after having killed his last wife. In Alfred Tennyson's 'Ulysses' (published 1842), the aged hero utters the monologue just before he embarks upon his last voyage.
- The presence of other characters (whom the speaker addresses) is indicated only through the words of the speaker. For example, in "My Last Duchess', the Duke says, 'That's my last Duchess painted on the wall … / Will't please you sit and look at her?'. In 'Ulysses', the presence of the sailors is indicated when Ulysses utters, 'Come, my friends, / 'Tis not too late to seek a newer world.'
- The setting and background are also indicated by the speaker. Thus we know we are in the palace of the Duke in Browning's poem. In Tennyson's dramatic monologue, Ulysses evokes a vivid picture of his kingdom, and later we

know we are at the seashore when he declares, 'There lies the port: the vessel puffs her sail: / There gloom the dark broad seas.'

- The chief purpose of a dramatic monologue is to reveal the character of the speaker. We understand the proud and cruel nature of the Duke in 'My Last Duchess' and Ulysses' insatiable thirst for adventure in Tennyson's poem.

Limerick

A limerick is a short and humorous (sometimes bawdy) poem consisting of five anapaestic (see page 27) lines. The rhyme scheme is AABBA:

The oldest recorded limerick is a thirteenth-century Latin prayer by Thomas Aquinas, while the oldest English ones date to the early eighteenth century. The origin of the name of this form is obscure and there are several theories about the same, one being that it is a reference to the Irish town of Limerick. The English poet Edward Lear popularised the form in his collection *A Book of Nonsense* (1846).

Two examples are given below. The authorship of the first is unknown; the second is by Edward Lear.

There once was a man from Nantucket A
Who kept all his cash in a bucket. A
    But his daughter, named Nan, B
    Ran away with a man B
And as for the bucket, Nantucket. A

There was a Young Lady whose chin A
Resembled the point of a pin: A
    So she had it made sharp, B
    And purchased a harp, B
And played several tunes with her chin. A

Lyric

The lyric is a short non-narrative poem which is a brief expression of mood or feeling. The term originally referred to Greek poetry composed to be sung to the accompaniment of the lyre or harp. The lyric was sung by a single person, unlike the choric song that was by a group of singers. In modern usage, a song is still often called a lyric; but in literature, the term is used to describe a poem that is not narrative in nature, and in which the poet is principally preoccupied with his thoughts or feelings. Used in a wider sense, the lyric includes different forms of poetry like the sonnet, elegy, ode and hymn.

Structure of a lyric

The lyric has three well-defined parts. In the first part, the poet states his emotion or the subject matter of the poem. In the second part, which forms the main body of the poem, the poet develops the emotion more fully. In the final part, the poet finds a balance in his emotions and reaches a reasonable conclusion. There is a lesson learnt or some comfort found. Usually, the final part of the poem tends to be philosophical or intellectual. The poem may end either with a smile or a sigh.

There are several examples to illustrate this three-fold structure of the lyric. John Milton begins 'On His Blindness' (circa 1655) with the emotion of deep sorrow at losing his eyesight and ends with the philosophical thought that 'They also serve who only stand and wait'. Percy Bysshe Shelley's 'Ode to the West Wind' (1820), which begins in pain and anguish ends with the consoling thought 'If Winter comes, can Spring be far behind?', after exploring the initial emotion through the middle verses.

Features of a lyric

- It is a short poem that does not tell a story, but makes a direct expression of emotion.
- It is essentially musical in nature.
- It is very subjective and expresses the varying emotions of the poet.
- It is well-structured, with the poet taking us through the different stages of his emotion.

Ode

An ode is a lyric poem of some length, usually of a serious or meditative nature, having an elevated style and formal stanzaic structure, and addressed to someone or something. It is of Greek origin. Originally it was a poem set to music and sung by a group of singers. The Greek ode had two forms, the Dorian ode and the Lesbian ode, with distinct structural differences. In England, the ode developed relatively free from classical influences.

Features of an ode

- It is lofty in subject matter and has an elevated tone and style. The subject is treated in a serious manner by the poet.
- The ode is a longer and more formal type of poem in comparison with the spontaneous lyric. The emotions in an ode are elaborately developed.
- The ode is addressed directly to a person, an object, or an abstract concept. Shelley's 'Ode to the West Wind' (published 1820) begins 'O wild West Wind …'. Keats's 'Ode on a Grecian Urn' (published 1820) is addressed thus: 'Thou still unravished bride of quietness …'
- The ode may also be written to commemorate an important public event, like victory in a war, the death of

an important person, or the inauguration of some large institution. Examples of such odes include Marvell's 'Upon Cromwell's Return from Ireland' and Tennyson's 'Ode on the Death of the Duke of Wellington' (1852).

Dorian ode

The Dorian ode is named after the district and dialect from which it originated. It was choric in nature and was sung to the accompaniment of dance. The structure of the poem was based on the movement of the dancers and had three distinct parts—the strophe, during the recitation of which the dancers moved from right to left; the antistrophe, when they turned from left to right; and the epode, in which the dancers stood still. This three-fold sequence could be repeated any number of times in the ode. The ancient Greek poet Pindar wrote so brilliantly in this particular form that it is also known as the **Pindaric ode**. Examples of this type of ode in English are Thomas Gray's 'The Bard' (1757) and 'The Progress of Poesy' (published 1759).

Lesbian ode

The Lesbian ode is named after the island of Lesbos, where it originated. It has a simpler form when compared to the Pindaric ode. Horace, the Latin poet, wrote odes in this form that were private and personal. His odes were homostrophic—that is, they were written in a single, repeated stanza form. Unlike the passionate Pindaric odes, **Horatian odes** are calmer and meditative in nature. The Horatian ode was very popular with English poets. Andrew Marvell's 'Upon Cromwell's Return from Ireland' (circa 1650), written in short four-lined stanzas having similar rhyme and metre, is the best example of this type of ode.

ENGLISH ODE

The English ode followed its own course, ignoring the classical models. The English ode has two forms: the regular and the irregular. The **regular ode** consists of similar stanzas and examples of this type of ode are those of Shelley and Keats. The **irregular ode** was introduced by Abraham Cowley in 1656. He imitated Pindar's style of writing odes but not the strophic form. Each stanza had its own length and rhyme scheme. The flexible nature of the irregular ode became very popular with the Romantics, and poets such as Wordsworth wrote in this form. His 'Ode: Intimations of Immortality' (published 1807) is an excellent example of an irregular ode.

Elegy

Originally, an elegy was a poem composed of **elegiac distiches** or **elegiac metre**. An elegiac distich was a pair of metrical lines of different lengths that expressed a complete idea. It consisted of a dactylic hexameter followed by a dactylic pentameter (see page 27 for a note on these terms). An elegy could be on any subject matter as long as it was written in this elegiac measure. In ancient Greece, the place of its origin, the term elegy covered themes such as love, war, politics, lamentations for the dead, and other subjects both sad and happy.

In present usage, an elegy is a poem of lament, written to mourn the death of an individual or to express grief at a tragic event. The English elegy does not use the ancient elegiac measure. Popular examples of an elegy include Thomas Gray's 'Elegy Written in a Country Churchyard' (1751) and Oliver Goldsmith's 'The Deserted Village' (1770).

Features of an elegy

- It is a poem of lament, mourning the death of a person, or the end of an era or way of life.

- It is not limited by form: the poet has the freedom to write in any form that he chooses.
- The tone adopted by the poet is dignified and solemn.
- The elegy is suitable for serious reflections on heavy topics such as life and death. Some poets use this form to digress and express their views on other subjects. In 'Lycidas' (1638), for example, Milton digresses to talk about the degradation of poetry and religion.
- Although the elegy is a poem of grief, it changes by the end to one of resignation, peace, or even joy, as the poet comes to terms with his loss.

Pastoral Elegy

It is a form of the elegy, in which the mourner and the one whose death is being mourned are represented as shepherds. (The Latin word for shepherd is *pastor*). The pastoral elegy originated in the work of the Sicilian Greek poet Theocritus (third century BCE). His *Idylls* and his *Epigrams* are the earliest known pastoral elegies. His 'Lament of Daphnis' is a well-known classical pastoral elegy, in which he mourns the death of the shepherd, Daphnis. Later, the Latin poet Virgil (70–19BCE) wrote his *Eclogues* and *Georgics* in this form. It was forgotten for several years until it was revived in Italy during the Renaissance. From there, it spread to Europe and England. Edmund Spenser's *The Shepherd's Calendar* (1579) is the first English pastoral elegy. His *Astrophel* (1595) is another important work in the same genre, written to mourn the death of his friend Sir Philip Sidney. Other important examples of this form include John Milton's 'Lycidas' (1638) and Matthew Arnold's *Thyrsis* (1865).

Features of a pastoral elegy

- The poet begins with an invocation to the muses, and frequently refers to various characters from mythology.

- All nature is shown as mourning the dead shepherd.
- The poet questions the guardian angels of the dead person and blames them for their negligence.
- There is a procession of mourners.
- The poet ponders on divine justice and reflects upon the evils of his own times.
- There is an elaborately descriptive passage which describes the flowers that are used to deck the hearse.
- The elegy concludes with a philosophic acceptance of death and the hope of meeting the departed again in heaven.

Idyll

An idyll is a short poem or an episode in a larger poem which describes a beautiful, rural scene or incident. It is not a poetic genre in the strictest sense: it is a brief poetic image (or a set of such images) and has no fixed form (they are usually passages within a larger lyric). The term is derived from the Greek word meaning 'little form' or 'little picture'.

The idyll is a vivid visual description of an idealised or serene environment. It often creates an impression of beauty, simplicity and harmony in nature and presents rural life in an idealised manner. The pastorals of Theocritus and Virgil (see page 19) may be considered idylls. Other examples include Henry Wadsworth Longfellow's 'The Village Blacksmith' (1840), Alfred Tennyson's *English Idylls, And Other Poems* (1874), and Robert Browning's Dramatic Idylls (1879).

Sonnet

A sonnet is a poem of fourteen iambic pentameter lines arranged in a specific rhyme scheme. The sonnet form originated in Italy in the thirteenth century. The word is derived from the

Italian *sonetto* meaning 'a little sound'. The sonnet has been an extremely popular form throughout English literary history, even to the modern day.

The Italian poet Petrarch (1304–74) wrote several sonnets in which he expressed his love for an idealised lady, Laura. Petrarch's poems were such a major influence on European literature that the classical form of the sonnet is known as the Petrarchan sonnet.

Petrarch ordered his poems into a sonnet cycle, *Il Canzoniere* (mid-fourteenth century). A **sonnet cycle** or a **sonnet sequence** is a collection of sonnets that are thematically linked and often show a progression in thought. The first major English sonnet cycle was Sir Philip Sidney's *Astrophel and Stella* (published 1591). Love was the most dominant theme of the sonnet during the Elizabethan age, but later practitioners such as John Donne and John Milton used the form to write on a variety of subjects, and ever since then the sonnet has been used for diverse subjects. Form and not theme is what defines a sonnet.

PETRARCHAN SONNET

The **Italian sonnet** or **Petrarchan sonnet** has two distinct parts—the 'octave' (the first eight lines) and the 'sestet' (the last six lines). The octave usually raises a question or poses a problem and the sestet serves as an answer or resolution to it. There is a well-marked pause between the octave and the sestet, which is known as the 'caesura'. The turn of thought after the caesura is known as the 'volta'.The octave rhymes *abbaabba*; the sestet rhymes *cdecde* (or a variant of it, such as *cdccdc*). The Petrarchan form was used by John Milton and Christina Rossetti, among others. Milton's poem 'On His Blindness' is an example of a Petrarchan sonnet.

I	When I consider how my light is spent	a
	E're half my days, in this dark world and wide,	b
	And that one Talent which is death to hide,	b
	Lodg'd with me useless, though my Soul more bent	a
	To serve therewith my Maker, and present	a
	My true account, least he returning chide,	b
	Doth God exact day-labour, light deny'd,	b
	I fondly ask; But patience to prevent	a
II ← (after "ask;")		
III	That murmur, soon replies, God doth not need	c
	Either man's work or his own gifts, who best	d
	Bear his mild yoke, they serve him best, his State	e
	Is Kingly. Thousands at his bidding speed	c
	And post o're Land and Ocean without rest:	d
	They also serve who only stand and wait.	e

I: octave (raises a question)
II: caesura (a pause) followed by volta (turn in thought)
III: sestet (resolution)

ENGLISH SONNET

In the first half of the sixteenth century, two Englishmen, Sir Thomas Wyatt and the Earl of Surrey, introduced the form to England. Surrey, and others after him, experimented with the classical Italian sonnet form till the structure became uniquely English. The English sonnet features three quatrains (four lines) and a concluding rhyming couplet: *abab cdcd efef gg*. This form was used so effectively by William Shakespeare that it is known today as the **Shakespearean sonnet**. Sonnet 129 from Shakespeare's sonnet sequence is a good example.

The expense of spirit in a waste of shame	a
Is lust in action; and till action, lust	b
Is perjur'd, murderous, bloody, full of blame,	a
Savage, extreme, rude, cruel, not to trust;	b
Enjoy'd no sooner but despised straight;	c

Past reason hunted; and no sooner had, d
Past reason hated, as a swallow'd bait, c
On purpose laid to make the taker mad: d
Mad in pursuit, and in possession so; e
Had, having, and in quest to have, extreme; f
A bliss in proof,—and prov'd, a very woe; e
Before, a joy propos'd; behind, a dream. f
All this the world well knows; yet none knows well g
To shun the heaven that leads men to this hell. g

An important variation of the English form was used by Edmund Spenser in his famous sonnet sequence *Amoretti* (published 1595). The **Spenserian sonnet**, too, has three quatrains and a rhyming couplet, but the quatrains are cleverly linked to each other with a connecting rhyme: *abab bcbc cdcd ee*. An example is Sonnet 75 from *Amoretti*.

One day I wrote her name upon the strand, a
But came the waves and washèd it away: b
Again I wrote it with a second hand, a
But came the tide and made my pains his prey. b
Vain man (said she) that dost in vain assay b
A mortal thing so to immortalise; c
For I myself shall like to this decay, b
And eke my name be wipèd out likewise. c
Not so (quod I); let baser things devise c
To die in dust, but you shall live by fame; d
My verse your virtues rare shall eternise, c
And in the heavens write your glorious name: d
Where, when as Death shall all the world subdue, e
Our love shall live, and later life renew. e

Epistle

An epistle is a letter in verse that is addressed to a friend or a patron. There are two types of epistles—on moral and philosophical themes, and on romantic themes. The classical model for the moral epistle is Horace's *Epistles,* and for the romantic epistle, Ovid's *Heroides*. During the Middle Ages, the Ovidian type was very popular. After the Renaissance, the Horatian kind had a greater impact. In England, Ben Jonson was the first to use the Horatian epistle in 'The Forest'. Alexander Pope was the greatest exponent of the form. His *Moral Essays* and 'Epistle to Dr Arbuthnot' are excellent examples of the epistle.

Satire

Satire could be defined as a work whose principal aim is to ridicule folly or vice. It has no definite literary form—it can exist in poetry, drama or prose. Samuel Johnson defined it as a mode 'in which wickedness and folly is censured'. The purpose of satire may be didactic; at times, however, it could be used to give vent to personal grievance. Some of the best examples of satire in English are Ben Jonson's *Volpone* (1606), John Dryden's *Absalom and Achitophel* (1681–82) and *Mac Flecknoe* (1682), Samuel Butler's *Hudibras* (1684) and Alexander Pope's *Dunciad* (1728–43). Examples of satire in the novel form are Miguel de Cervantes's *Don Quixote* (1605–15) and Jonathan Swift's *Gulliver's Travels* (1726). While Jonson satirised certain types of people in society, Swift pointed out the defects of all mankind. Dryden made use of satire to mock at his political opponents, and Pope mainly used it to make fun of his critics and rivals.

The plays of the fourth century BCE Greek playwright Aristophanes are the earliest known satires. Satire was quite popular in Latin literature too, with writers like Horace, Persius and Juvenal excelling in it. These writers served as models to the satirists of the Renaissance and later periods. Satire became very popular during the neoclassical period in England.

Satire may be broadly divided into two categories: Horatian satire and the Juvenalian satire. **Horatian satire** is relaxed and more tolerant. Horace used satire as a vehicle to gently laugh at human weaknesses. On the other hand, Juvenal used satire as a weapon to attack his adversaries and to condemn vice. Consequently, **Juvenalian satire** is harsh and cynical.

The Elements of Poetry

Rhyme

We may define rhyme as the sameness of sound, especially in the endings of verse lines (for example: may, day; bright, might). Such matching sounds in lines of verse create a melodic pattern. Rhyme is pleasing to the human ear. It is also a mnemonic device that can help people learn and remember things easily. For example, in order to help us remember the number of days in any month, the following rhyme is very useful—

Thirty days hath September,
April, June and November.
All the rest have thirty-one
Except February alone,
And that has twenty-eight days clear,
And twenty-nine in a leap year.

There are many different kinds of rhyme. Look at the following lines of verse.

The curfew tolls the knell of parting day,
The lowing herd wind slowly o'er the *lea*,
The plowman homeward plods his weary way,
And leaves the world to darkness and to *me*.

Jack and *Jill* went up a *hill*,
To fetch a pail of water.
Jack fell *down* and broke his *crown*
And Jill came tumbling after.

A **masculine rhyme** consists of a single stressed syllable that bears the rhyme. For example, in the above lines, 'day' and 'way' are masculine rhymes, as are 'lea' and 'me'.

A **feminine rhyme** consists of a stressed syllable followed by an unstressed syllable, with the latter bearing the rhyming sound. For example, 'water' and 'after' are feminine rhymes.

End rhyme occurs when the rhyming words are placed at the ends of lines; for example, 'day' and 'way', and 'water' and 'after'. (The **rhyme scheme** of a poem is the pattern of end rhymes in it.)

Internal rhyme occurs when the rhyming words fall within a line; for example, 'Jill' and 'hill', and 'down' and 'crown'.

Exact rhyme is the use of identical rhyming sounds, as in 'Jill' and 'hill', and 'down' and 'crown'.

Approximate rhyme or **slant rhyme** is the use of sounds that are similar but not identical; for example, the pair 'prove' and 'glove'.

Eye rhymes appeal to the eye, not the ear. They are words that are spelt similarly but pronounced differently. For example, 'flow' and 'now', 'home' and 'come'. Another example is 'thirty-one' and 'alone' in the poem above about the days in a month.

Metre

The term 'metre' refers to the pattern of stresses in a line of verse. In English, every syllable in a word is either stressed or unstressed. A **metrical foot** is a combination of a strong stress and an associated weak stress or stresses. An iambic foot, for example, will contain an unstressed syllable followed by a stressed syllable. Take a look at the iambic units in the following line—

T̆he cúr | f̆ew tólls | t̆he knéll | ŏf pár | t̆ing dáy

In the English language, there are five standard feet.

Foot	Adjective	Stress pattern
iamb	iambic	unstressed-stressed
anapaest	anapaestic	unstressed-unstressed-stressed
trochee	trochaic	stressed-unstressed
dactyl	dactylic	stressed-unstressed-unstressed
spondee	spondaic	stressed-stressed

Examples of each are as follows—

Foot	Example
iamb	I **wand** | ered **lone** | ly **as** | a **cloud**
anapaest	I am **mon** | arch of **all** | I sur**vey**
trochee	**Ty**ger, | **Ty**ger, | **burn**ing | **bright**
dactyl	**Can**non to | **right** of them
spondee	**Break**, **break**, | **break**

A metrical line is named after the number of feet in it.

monometer	one foot	dimeter	two feet
trimeter	three feet	tetrameter	four feet
pentameter	five feet	hexameter	six feet
heptameter	seven feet	octameter	eight feet

Hence, the following line

The cur | few tolls | the knell | of par | ting day

is said to be in 'iambic pentameter', since it has five feet, each of which is an iamb (an unstressed syllable followed by a stressed syllable).

An **alexandrine** is a line of poetry written in iambic hexameter. The line is made up of six feet, each containing one weakly stressed syllable followed by one strongly stressed syllable. It gets its name from old French poems about Alexander the Great. Alexandrines never became popular in England. Edmund Spenser used them as the concluding line of each stanza of *The Faerie Queene*. The best example of an alexandrine is by Alexander Pope, who illustrates its potential to slow down the flow of a poem—

A needless alexandrine ends the song
That like | a woun | ded snake, | drags its | slow length | along.

Stanza forms

A stanza is a group of lines that form a unit in verse. The stanza in a poem is similar to a paragraph in prose. Each new stanza deals with a fresh turn of thought.

Various types of stanzas are differentiated by the number of lines in them, the number of feet in each line, or by their metrical pattern. Some of the most well-known stanza forms are listed below.

A **couplet** is a stanza of two lines. The **heroic couplet** is a stanza of two iambic pentameter lines that rhyme together. It is called 'heroic' as the couplet (whether it rhymed or not) was used extensively in heroic literature (see page 59). The following is an example from Pope's *The Rape of the Lock*.

The Fair ones feel such Maladies as these,
When each new Night-Dress gives a new Disease.

The **tercet** is a stanza of three lines. The **terza rima** is a series of interlocking tercets with the following rhyme scheme: *aba bcb cdc*. This measure was adopted by Dante in his *Divine Comedy*. The following example is from Shelley's 'Ode to the West Wind'.

O wild West Wind, thou breath of Autumn's being a
  Thou from whose unseen presence the leaves dead b
Are driven like ghosts from an enchanter fleeing, a
  Yellow, and black, and pale, and hectic red, b
Pestilence-stricken multitudes! O thou c
  Who chariotest to their dark wintry bed b
The wingèd seeds, where they lie cold and low, c
  Each like a corpse within its grave, until d
Thine azure sister of the Spring shall blow c

A **quatrain** is a stanza of four lines. Gray's 'Elegy Written in a Country Churchyard' is written in quatrains. Another example of this stanza form may be seen in Edward FitzGerald's *Rubáiyát of Omar Khayyám*, a quatrain from which is given below.

Come, fill the Cup, and in the fire of Spring
Your Winter-garment of Repentance fling:
The Bird of Time has but a little way
To flutter—and the Bird is on the Wing.

A **pentastich** is a stanza of five lines.

A **sestet** is a stanza of six lines. The second part of a Petrarchan sonnet (see page 21) is known as a sestet. It can have various rhyme schemes such as *cde cde, dcd cdc*, and so on.

A **septet** is a stanza of seven lines. The **rhyme royal** is a stanza form of seven lines of iambic pentameter with the rhyme scheme *ababbcc*. It is so named due to its use by King James I of England. It is also known as a **Chaucerian stanza** since it was Chaucer who popularised it. The following rhyme royal is taken from Chaucer's *Troilus and Criseyde*.

The double sorwe of Troilus to tellen,	a
That was the king Priamus sone of Troye,	b
In lovinge, how his aventures fellen	a
Fro wo to wele, and after out of Ioye,	b
My purpos is, er that I parte fro ye.	b
Thesiphone, thou help me for tendyte	c
Thise woful vers, that wepen as I wryte!	c

An **octastich** is a stanza of eight lines. The **ottava rima** is an eight-line iambic pentameter stanza rhyming *abababcc*. This stanza is of Italian origin and was originally used for long poems dealing with heroic subjects. One of the earliest poets who used this was Boccaccio. The following example is from Byron's *Don Juan*.

'Go, little book, from this my solitude! a
I cast thee on the waters—go thy ways! b
And if, as I believe, thy vein be good, a
The world will find thee after many days.' b
When Southey's read, and Wordsworth understood, a
I can't help putting in my claim to praise— b
The four first rhymes are Southey's every line: c
For God's sake, reader! take them not for mine. c

The **Spenserian stanza** is a stanza of nine iambic lines, in which the first eight are pentameters and the last is a hexameter (that is, an alexandrine, see page 27). This verse form was created by Edmund Spenser for his epic poem *The Faerie Queene*. The rhyme scheme of these lines is *ababbcbcc*. The following lines constitute the first verse of the poem.

Lo I the man, whose Muse whilome did maske, a
As time her taught, in lowly Shepheards weeds, b
Am now enforst a far vnfitter taske, a
For trumpets sterne to chaunge mine Oaten reeds, b
And sing of Knights and Ladies gentle deeds; b
Whose prayses hauing slept in silence long, c
Me, all too meane, the sacred Muse areeds b
To blazon broad emongst her learned throng: c
Fierce warres and faithfull loues shall moralize my song. c

TYPES OF VERSE

Verse is metrical writing, as opposed to prose which does not follow metrical patterns. Verse could also refer to a single metrical line in a poetic composition. A stanza is made up of lines of verse, of which there are several types.

Blank verse is poetry written in unrhymed iambic pentameter lines. As it sounds very much like ordinary spoken English, it is often used in drama. Some of the great poets who have used blank verse in poetry are William Wordsworth, Robert Browning and W.H. Auden.

Free verse is poetry which is not written in a regular metrical pattern. Instead of having metrical feet, free verse has a rhythm that suits its meaning and uses the sounds of spoken language in lines of different lengths. This type of versification was very popular in the twentieth century. Notable practitioners include Walt Whitman and Allen Ginsberg.

The **villanelle** is a nineteen-line French verse form, consisting of five tercets followed by a quatrain. The three lines in each of the first five stanzas rhyme *aba*. The final quatrain rhymes *abaa*. In addition to this, it has two refrains formed by repeating line 1 in lines 6, 12 and 18, and by repeating line 3 in lines 9, 15 and 19. An example of a villanelle is Dylan Thomas's 'Do Not Go Gentle into That Good Night'.

Figures of Speech

IMAGERY

Imagery is descriptive language that produces pictures in a person's mind. It is one of the elements that gives poetry its forcefulness. Poets use words to help us see the things they are describing from a fresh point of view. Images in poetry can appeal to more than one of our senses. An image can help us see colour or movement. At times it can help us hear a sound, smell an odour, feel texture or even taste a flavour.

Keats's 'Ode to a Nightingale' is full of sensuous images—

> O for a draught of vintage! that hath been
> Cool'd a long age in the deep-delvèd earth,
> Tasting of Flora and the country-green,
> Dance, and Provençal song, and sunburnt mirth!
> O for a beaker full of the warm South!
> Full of the true, the blushful Hippocrene,
> With beaded bubbles winking at the brim,
> And purple-stainèd mouth;

In the above lines, Keats uses an image that mixes two different senses—that of sight and taste. This is known as '**synaesthesia**' which is derived from a word of Greek origin meaning 'feel together'. Keats makes use of an image that appeals to our sense of sight in order to describe the taste of wine. He describes the taste of wine in terms of colour, action, song, sensation and feeling.

An image can appeal to our feelings too. A poet can use images in such a way as to make us feel the joy, grief, wonder or disgust that he is talking about. See how the following lines—the first from Wordsworth, the next by Shelley—arouses our emotions through an image.

My heart leaps up when I behold
A rainbow in the sky.

I fall upon the thorns of life! I bleed!

Simile and Metaphor

Similes and metaphors are common figures of speech used by a poet to embellish his work. A **simile** is a figure of speech in which two objects are compared by using the words 'like' or 'as'. See, for example, these lines by Byron and Burns, respectively.

She walks in beauty, like the night
Of cloudless climes and starry skies

My love is like a red, red rose,
That's newly sprung in June

In a **metaphor**, the connective 'like' or 'as' is omitted. For example in the sentence 'She has a heart of stone', the author wishes to state that the two objects being compared (heart, stone) have the same qualities.

Personification

Personification is the attribution of human qualities to something that is not human. For example, Keats compares the Grecian urn to a bride and personifies it by addressing it thus—

Thou still unravished bride of quietness,
Thou foster child of silence and slow time

Here is another example from Shakespeare's *As You Like It*.

Blow, blow thou winter wind.
Thou art not so unkind
As man's ingratitude.
Thy tooth is not so keen,
Because thou art not seen,
Although thy breath be rude.

The wind, which is not human, is given human attributes such as teeth and breath and the characteristic of being rude.

Onomatopoeia

Onomatopoeia is a figure of speech in which words contain the sounds they describe; for example, 'hiss' or 'bang'. Here is an excellent example from 'The Highwayman' by Alfred Noyes—

Over the cobbles he *clattered* and *clashed* in the dark inn-yard …
Tlot-tlot, in the frosty silence! *Tlot-tlot*, in the echoing night!

Alliteration

Alliteration is the repetition of similar sounds in several words. The repetition of the /k/ sound in the line 'Over the ***c***obbles he ***c***lattered and ***c***lashed …' is an example of alliteration. Alliteration may also be seen in Edgar Allan Poe's 'The Raven'—

The **s**ilken **s**ad un***c***ertain ru**s**tling of each purple curtain.

Another example of alliteration is from the short story 'The Dead' by James Joyce—

> ***H**is **s**oul **s**wooned **s**lowly a**s** **h**e **h**eard the **s**now ***f**alling*
> ***f**aintly through the univer**s**e and ***f**aintly ***f**alling ...

Apostrophe

An apostrophe is a figure of speech in which a speaker directly addresses an absent person or a personified quality, object or idea. Keats opens his poem 'Ode on a Grecian Urn' with an apostrophe that addresses the urn: 'Thou still unravished bride of quietness ...'. This figure of speech is often used in poetry and speeches to add emotional intensity.

Hyperbole

A hyperbole is an exaggeration or overstatement. It is often used either for heightened seriousness or for comic effect. Here is an example from Pope's *The Rape of the Lock*.

> Sol thro' white curtains shot a tim'rous ray,
> And op'd those *eyes that* must *eclipse the day*

Oxymoron

An oxymoron is a figure of speech that fuses two contradictory or opposing ideas; for example, 'freezing fire' or 'happy grief'. In Book I of *Paradise Lost*, Milton uses the oxymoron 'darkness visible' when describing Hell.

Allegory

An allegory is a story which has layers of meaning—the characters and events of the surface story suggest a deeper level of meaning or represent other things by way of an extended metaphor. The characters, settings and events in an allegory may stand for abstract or moral concepts, or may parallel other characters (people), settings and events.

It is similar to a **fable** and a **parable** which are moral stories that are used to illustrate truths. The word 'allegory' is derived from the Greek *ἀλληγορία* ('*allēgoría*') which means 'speaking otherwise'. Examples of an allegories are John Bunyan's *The Pilgrim's Progress*, John Dryden's *Absalom and Achitophel* and *Mac Flecknoe,* Jonathan Swift's *The Battle of the Books*, and George Orwell's *Animal Farm*.

ALLUSION

An allusion is a reference to another literary work or person or event. An author uses allusions to enrich his work and give it a more profound meaning. Allusions may include references to people or events, references to the author's own life, or references to other literary works. For example, when one calls a person a 'Scrooge', one is referring to Ebenezer Scrooge, a miserly character from *A Christmas Carol* by Charles Dickens (and thereby implying that the person is stingy). Pope and Dryden make use of several allusions to events and people of their age in their works. The title of William Faulkner's novel *The Sound and the Fury* is an allusion to a line from William Shakespeare's *Macbeth* ('Life's … / … a tale / Told by an idiot, full of sound and fury, / Signifying nothing.').

ANTICLIMAX

An anticlimax could be defined as a disappointing or ludicrous conclusion to a series of noble or serious events. Somerset Maugham's short stories (for example, 'The Man with the Scar') usually end in an anticlimax.

CLICHÉ

A cliché is an expression or word that is overused; for example, 'selling like hotcakes', 'avoid like the plague', 'with flying colours', or 'another feather in his cap'. Writing that uses too many idiomatic expressions may be said to be clichéd.

Euphemism

A euphemism may be defined as an inoffensive or indirect word or expression used in place of one that is considered unpleasant or shocking. For example, one says 'he passed away' instead of 'he died'.

The term originally referred to the elaborate and ornate style of writing which was introduced by John Lyly in his works *Euphues, the Anatomy of Wyt* (1578) and *Euphues and his England* (1580).

Irony

Irony is a literary device that refers to the contrast between the surface meaning and the underlying meaning of what is being said. Irony may be of the verbal, dramatic or situational kind.

Example of **verbal irony**: All the characters in the play *Othello* (especially the protagonist) use the epithet 'honest' to describe the lying, dishonest Iago.

Example of **dramatic irony**: This is a situation created when the audience knows the truth about something which the character does not know. In *Romeo and Juliet*, Romeo kills himself thinking that Juliet is dead, while the audience knows that she is merely unconscious.

Example of **situational irony**: In Coleridge's 'The Rime of the Ancient Mariner', the protagonist is surrounded by water on all four sides, yet hc cannot quench his overpowering thirst as the water is not potable.

Metonymy

It is a figure of speech in which an attribute of a thing or a name is used to substitute the thing itself. For example, 'the Crown' is used to refer to the king, and 'Shakespeare' is used to refer to Shakespeare's works.

Paradox

A paradox is a statement that apparently contradicts itself. An example of a paradox may be found in George Orwell's novel *Animal Farm*, in which the animals adopt the law 'All animals are equal, but some animals are more equal than others'. Yet another example of paradox is when Hamlet states 'I must be cruel to be kind'.

Synecdoche

It is a figure of speech in which a part of a thing is used to denote the entire object or the whole is used to denote a part. For example, when one says 'India lost the match', one means that the Indian team lost the match. Here, a whole (India) is used to denote a part (a small group of Indians who constitute a sports team). Again, when one says 'I need more hands for this task', one means that more workers are needed. A part (hand) is used to denote a whole (a person). Another example of synecdoche from everyday life is using the word 'plastic' for credit card (substituting the material from which the card is made for the card itself). In *The Rape of the Lock*, when Pope says 'all Arabia breathes from yonder box', he is using synecdoche to mean 'the perfumes of Arabia'.

It is common to confuse synecdoche with metonymy. The difference lies in the fact that in a synecdoche, a part is used to represent the whole, or a whole used for a part, whereas in metonymy, there is a substitution of a word or a phrase for another word or phrase that is loosely associated with it. The statement 'Rashtrapati Bhavan issued a statement' means that the office of the President of India issued a statement, and is an example of metonymy—Rashtrapati Bhavan is associated with the President of India, but is not a part of the actual person. 'She has the best set of wheels' and 'She has the best ride' both mean 'She has the best car', but the first is an example of synecdoche (wheels, part, for car, whole) while the second is an example of metonymy (ride, associated idea, for car).

Transferred epithet

Also known as **hypallage**, which is derived from a Greek word meaning 'exchange', a transferred epithet is a figure of speech in which the epithet is transferred from the noun it actually describes to another noun that is closely associated with it in the sentence.

In Thomas Gray's 'Elegy Written in a Country Churchyard', the poet writes 'The plowman homeward plods his weary way'. The way is not weary; it is the plowman who is weary. Thus, the application of the word 'weary' to way is a transferred epithet.

Pun

A pun is a play on the multiple meanings of a word, or the use of two words that sound alike but have different meanings. Shakespeare's plays are rich in puns. In *Hamlet*, when King Claudius, (who murdered Hamlet's father, married his mother, and crowned himself king) addresses Hamlet as 'my cousin … and my son', Hamlet remarks, 'A little more than kin, and less than kind' (meaning, 'I am more kin to you now than before—as both nephew and stepson—but I am no kin to you with regard to our temperaments, or in my emotions towards you'). The opening lines of Richard III is another famous example—

> Now is the winter of our discontent
> Made glorious summer by this sun of York

The new king is the son of the Duke of York, and his emblem is the sun.

2

Drama

Drama is a form of literature that has plot, characters, dialogue and action, and is meant to be performed on the stage. It is one of the oldest literary forms, along with poetry. Although no one knows exactly how drama originated, there is evidence of its existence in almost every civilisation.

Western drama originated in ancient Greece. Invariably, the earliest forms of drama have a deep connection with religious ceremonies. Greek drama had its origin in the festivals held in honour of Dionysus (the god of fertility, revelry and wine). In ancient Rome too, drama formed a part of religious ceremonies. English drama (which came into existence much later), too, had its origin in the church.

Drama differs from other literary forms in that it depends on the stage for its true existence. Therefore, the dramatist's art has always been shaped by the theatrical conditions of his times. As a result, the study of drama is interwoven with the study of theatre.

Traditionally, drama has been broadly classified under two main headings—tragedy and comedy. From the beginning of the modern age, various forms and subtypes of drama that transcended these two categories came into existence. However, these two broad categories still influence the way we study and attempt to classify drama.

Tragedy

The term 'tragedy' is broadly applied to dramatic representations of serious actions which have a disastrous end for the protagonist, who is of noble birth or high rank. Greek tragedy is one of the earliest forms of drama. The earliest known tragedies in Western art are the Greek plays of Aeschylus (circa 525–455BCE), Sophocles (circa 497–405BCE), and Euripides (circa 480–406BCE), and the later Roman tragedies of Seneca (circa 4BCE–65CE). In English literature, the Elizabethan and Jacobean periods witnessed the production of the finest works of English tragedy by dramatists such as Christopher Marlowe (1564–93), William Shakespeare (1564–1616), and John Webster (circa 1580–1634).

Numerous writers, critics and philosophers have focused on tragedy as a form and on its themes. The distinctive features of early Greek plays are familiar to us through the Greek philosopher Aristotle's *Poetics* (circa 335BCE). With the passage of time, there was a change in the concept of tragedy. In the twentieth century, tragedy has captured the attention of people by concentrating on the fate of ordinary people.

Comedy

The word 'comedy' is derived from the Greek word κῶμος ('*komos*'), meaning 'revel' or 'merrymaking'. Like tragedy, comedy too has been associated with religion and Dionysus. According to Aristotle, comedy deals with the everyday activities of ordinary people. There is no serious or dangerous action, and the story concludes happily for the protagonists. Comedy deals with some defect or ugliness that is not serious or destructive. The concept of comedy, too, has undergone changes with the passage of time.

There are three distinct periods in classical Greek comedy—old, middle and new. Aristophanes (circa 446–386BCE) belonged to the old period and his comedies were marked by buffoonery, satire and social commentaries. The most important writer of the middle period was Antiphanes (circa 408–334BCE). During that period, the plays were noted for burlesque. Menander (circa 341–290BCE) belonged to the new period and was the most influential of the Greek comedy writers. The new comedy focused on the amorous intrigues of young lovers and did not bother with social issues. Though Menander was not an excellent playwright, he had a great impact upon the Roman comedy writers Plautus (circa 254–184BCE) and Terence (circa 195–159BCE), who in turn influenced the English writers of the Middle Ages. In England, comedy began by imitating the classical style of the ancient Greeks and Romans. Nicholas Udall's *Ralph Roister Doister* (written circa 1553) is considered to be the first English comedy.

Dramatic design

Before examining the different types of drama, a look at some of its technical aspects would be useful. Every dramatic narrative arises out of some **conflict** (an opposition between persons, ideas or interests). This conflict leads to the development of the plot. The German novelist and playwright Gustav Freytag (1816–95) pointed out that the plot of a play may be represented as a pyramidal structure containing five main divisions.

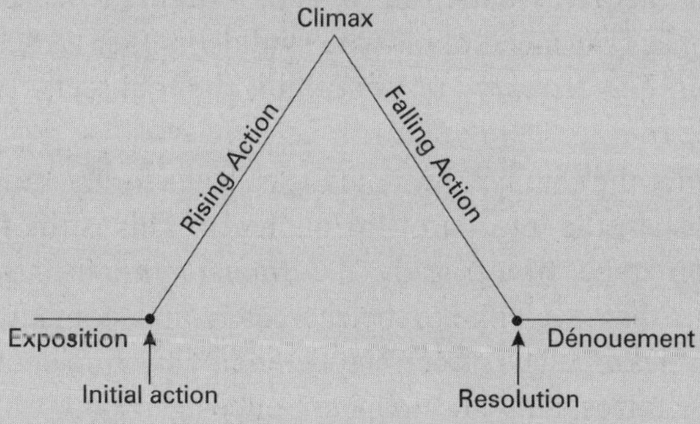

The play begins with **exposition**, which conveys essential background information to the audience or the readers. Such information may introduce characters, set the scene and talk about the incidents that have occurred immediately prior to the beginning of the main plot. An initial incident, either a physical or a mental action, sets off the conflict of the drama. Sometimes the initial incident is rolled into the exposition and it becomes difficult to separate the two. For instance, in *Hamlet*, the appearance of the ghost on the battlements of the castle kick-starts the entire action of the play.

The plot thickens in the **rising action** stage. In both tragedy and comedy, there is conflict, and the audience is in a state of suspense as to its ultimate outcome. The **climax** is the point of greatest interest in the play, and is often the turning point of the play with regard to the fate of the protagonist. In a tragedy, the climax determines that the protagonist will have an unhappy ending, while in a comedy it is the opposite. In modern drama, the climax usually appears only towards the end of the play. In Shakespearean drama, however, the climax is usually placed somewhere close to the middle of the play. For example, in *Julius Caesar,* the climax is the assassination scene (act III, scene i); in *Othello,* it occurs when Othello is finally convinced of his wife's infidelity (act IV, scene i), and in *The Merchant of Venice,* it is the trial scene (act IV, scene i).

Once the climax is over, it is a challenge for the dramatist to sustain the interest of the audience. This is the **falling action** stage. In a tragedy, the dramatist might introduce events that give hope to the characters; in a comedy, fresh obstacles might be placed before them. These incidents help revive uncertainty and suspense once again. For example, in *King Lear,* when Edmund revokes his command that Lear and Cordelia should be put to death, we are filled with fresh hope for the protagonists. Similarly, when the Friar in *Romeo and Juliet* gives a new plan to Juliet for her successful union with Romeo, the audience begins to hope for the best. In *The Merchant of Venice,* the quarrel over the rings creates new interest.

The final section of the dramatic design is the **dénouement**. Here, all the lines of the story are gathered together and tied up neatly. The resolution solves the protagonist's main problem or source of conflict. A tragedy often ends in a catastrophe; for example, the death of all the major characters in the final scene of *Hamlet*. In comedy, the protagonist's situation improves significantly from what it was at the beginning; for example, in *Twelfth Night*, Viola is able to shed her disguise and marry Orsino.

The conclusion should be a natural outcome of the previous events. In this context, Aristotle had written: 'It is … evident that the unravelling of the plot, no less than its complication, must arise out of the plot itself; it must not be brought about by the *deus ex machina*'. A ***deus ex machina*** was a device used in Greek drama through which the character of a god was lowered on the stage by a machine, in order to get the protagonist out of difficulties or to untangle the plot. In modern drama, this could refer to any form of contrived ending, such as the death of the antagonist by a timely accident or the appearance of a lost will.

Freytag's analysis of dramatic design applies primarily to classical and Shakespearean drama. Modern drama usually does not fit into neat patterns like the above.

Classical Greek Tragedy

Greek tragedy flourished during the fifth century BCE, which is regarded as the 'Golden Age' of Greek literature. Aeschylus, Sophocles and Euripides were the three great dramatists who wrote during this period. The plays were performed in huge amphitheatres, the largest ones having a seating capacity of more than 15,000 people. The performers had to enact the plays in a shallow 'speaking place' at the centre of the semicircular theatre. The shallowness of the speaking place did not give much scope for any mass scenes. The dramatist had to keep these restrictions in mind when writing his plays, which resulted in certain features peculiar to Greek tragedy.

IMAGE B: This amphitheater, located in Epidaurus (Greece), was built in the fourth century BCE, and can seat up to 14,000 people.

Features of a Greek tragedy

- The subject matter was limited by the religious angle of drama. The theme of a Greek tragedy had to be familiar to the audience, as any unknown story would have been difficult to understand due to the vastness of the theatres. As a result, the dramatist had to choose his stories from Greek mythology, which was well known to all citizens. The audience could then easily follow the main storyline of the play.

- The characters wore padded costumes, platform heels and large masks (depicting a character's state of mind) in order to make themselves more visible to the huge audience. The masks placed a severe restriction on the dramatist as there was absolutely no scope for any quick changes in disposition. The costume also prevented any abrupt action. This led to the creation of stereotypes.
- The distance of the actors from the audience prevented rapid exchanges of dialogue, low tones and changing inflections. Dialogue, as a result, had to be rhetorical and not conversational in nature.
- Since action was restricted, all scenes that required action (such as battles) were narrated.
- A unique feature of Greek tragedy is the **chorus**. The chorus was a group of men, wearing masks, who sang and performed dancelike movements. They served as commentators on the action and reflected the moral, social and religious attitudes of the age.
- Since the action of the drama was carried on from the beginning to the end in the presence of the chorus—who served as witnesses—the dramatist had to follow the **three unities** of time, place and action. Unity of time requires that the time represented in the play should be limited to the two or three hours taken to enact the play, or, at the most, not more than a single day of either twelve or twenty-four hours. The unity of place dictated that the entire action should take place in one location, and the unity of action necessitated the restriction of the action to one single plot.
- As the story was known to the audience, there was no scope for suspense in Greek tragedy. But what it lost by way of suspense was amply made up by the presence of **dramatic irony**. Dramatic irony could be defined as the

gap between the characters' ignorance of future events and the audience's knowledge of the same.

Any study of classical Greek tragedy is incomplete without Aristotle's definition of tragedy as being 'the imitation of an action that is serious and also, as having magnitude, complete in itself … incorporating incidents arousing pity and fear, wherewith to accomplish the catharsis of such emotions'. The tragic hero, who would be able to evoke pity and fear, could only be one who is of noble birth or high rank. He should be a virtuous character, who makes an error in judgment (referred to by the Greek term **hamartia**) which is responsible for a reversal in his fortunes (the Greek term for this reversal being **peripeteia**). This is accompanied by **anagnorisis**, or the moment when a critical truth is discovered or some insight is gained by the protagonist. The effect of the resolution of tragic drama on the audience is one of **catharsis** (the purging of emotional tensions). Tragedy, by arousing powerful emotions in people, has a therapeutic effect by causing a purgation of such emotions.

Aeschylus' *Agamemnon* and *The Eumenides* (both 458BCE), Euripides' *Medea* (431BCE), and Sophocles' *Oedipus the King* (429BCE) are some of the best surviving Greek tragedies.

Senecan or Revenge Tragedy

Senecan tragedy refers to a set of plays of the classical Roman writer Seneca, a first century CE Stoic Roman philosopher and dramatist. Seneca adapted tragedies from the Greeks, the most well-known among them being *Phaedra*, *Thyestes*, and *Oedipus*. The plays feature bloody revenge and supernatural elements. Senecan tragedy greatly influenced Elizabethan revenge tragedy as well as French neoclassical tragedy.

In a revenge tragedy, the protagonist concentrates on taking revenge upon those who wronged him. It was made very popular during the Elizabethan Age by Thomas Kyd (circa 1558–94), whose play *The Spanish Tragedy* (circa 1587) is the best example of the revenge tradition in English drama.

Features of a revenge tragedy

- The theme of these plays is usually revenge, and the morally upright protagonist is pitted against cunning antagonists who have committed an unpunished crime.
- Revenge tragedies often feature declamatory and emotionally charged speeches. Soliloquies are also very common.
- Although these plays feature murder, torture and other horrific incidents, most scenes of violence are either only reported (not enacted on the stage) or depicted through a 'dumb show'.
- Another common feature of this type of drama is **stichomythia**, the rapid exchange of dialogue, giving a sense of argument. Here is an example from *Hamlet* (act III, scene iv)—

  Queen: Hamlet, thou hast thy father much offended.
  Hamlet: Mother, you have my father much offended.
  Queen: Come, come, you answer with an idle tongue.
  Hamlet: Go, go, you question with a wicked tongue.
- Madness (real or feigned), murder, disguise and ghosts of murder victims are common elements.

These plays, when they were introduced into England, had a strong influence on English drama. Nearly all of the above features can be seen in the first English tragedy, *Gorboduc* (1561), by Thomas Norton and Thomas Sackville. Thomas Kyd's *The Spanish Tragedy* deviated from Seneca in that Kyd presented all the violence on the stage. William Shakespeare's *Hamlet* (1603) and John Webster's *The White Devil* (1612) and *The Duchess of Malfi* (1612–13), too, were influenced by the Senecan revenge tradition.

Neoclassical Tragedy

In the sixteenth century, Italian and French dramatists modified the ancient Greek and the Senecan models and established a form of neoclassical tragedy, which differed from classical tragedy in a few points.

Features of neoclassical tragedy

- Like the classicists, the neoclassicists also dealt with the great legends of the past. The chief characters belonged to an elevated background and were far above ordinary human beings.
- In neoclassical tragedy, prominent place is given to romantic love between a hero and a heroine. This was conspicuously absent in the tragedies of ancient Greece and Rome. The classical writers were of the opinion that the introduction of romantic love would mar the dignity of the hero and the high seriousness of the narrative.
- The neoclassical writers dropped the chorus from their plays as they felt it was awkward and clumsy. Instead, they introduced the concept of the confidant who had little to do with the action except to listen to the confessions of the protagonists and offer sympathy.
- The language used is elevated and poetic.
- The playwrights made no attempt to mirror daily life in their plays.

Pierre Corneille's *Medée* (1635) and *Le Cid* (1636) and Jean Racine's *Andromaque* (circa 1667) and *Phèdre* (circa 1677) are the best examples of neoclassical tragedy.

The origin and growth of drama in England

The cradle of British drama is said to be the altar. Priests, in order to reach out to their congregations, began to perform plays in Latin called **mystery plays** and **miracle**

plays. This form of religious drama was popular in the Middle Ages. While mystery plays dramatised Biblical events, miracle plays depicted the lives of saints. These plays were presented as a part of the Roman Catholic church service. Gradually, they lost the approval of the church and were taken up by various guilds of tradesmen, who performed the plays on the streets or in public squares. The plays were now written in English and the verses were rough and vigorous. By the fourteenth century, these plays were developed into elaborate cycles representing various Biblical episodes, from the creation of the world to the crucifixion of Christ. At times, comic scenes (for example, exchanges between Noah and his wife) were included.

Morality plays represented yet another type of didactic drama which reflected medieval philosophy. Morality plays were essentially sermons that were dramatised. The theme of these plays was the conflict between good and evil. Since the theme was abstract, the treatment was allegorical, with characters representing Virtue, Poverty, Knowledge or Ignorance. *Everyman* (late fifteenth century) is the best surviving example of a morality play. In it, the character Everyman is summoned by Death and is deserted by his friends, Goods, Knowledge, Strength and Beauty. Only one friend—Good Deeds—is prepared to take the journey with him.

The **interlude** was a short entertainment put on between the courses of a feast or between the acts of a longer play. These were mostly sketches that were non-religious in nature. Interludes were popular in England in the medieval and early modern periods. A well-known example is *The Play of the Weather* (1533) by John Heywood.

Romantic Tragedy

In England, an independent type of drama began to develop, which was free from the influence of Seneca and neoclassicism. This is known as Romantic drama. Shakespeare's great tragedies, such as *Othello* (circa 1603), *Macbeth* (circa 1605), and *King Lear* (circa 1606), are all examples of Romantic tragedies.

Features of a romantic tragedy

- Like neoclassical tragedy, romantic tragedy, too, has men of high birth or rank as its protagonists. But these men are shown to interact with and move amidst common characters of lower social rank.
- The dialogue is predominantly poetical, although it sometimes lapses into the colloquial and the familiar. Romantic tragedy thus combines the idealistic with the realistic.
- The unities of time and place were totally abandoned, and the unity of action was interpreted very differently. The action usually contains a main plot and one or more subplots—the unity of action lies in the clever interweaving of all the plots by the dramatist.
- In Elizabethan tragedy, a lot of violence and movement is shown on the stage. While neoclassical tragedy is mostly narrative, romantic tragedy is a drama of action.
- Humorous scenes are included, both to relieve the intensity of the tragic scenes and to provide a sharp ironical contrast.
- Neoclassical tragedy deviated from classical tragedy by including romantic love as a part of its subject. This is continued in romantic tragedy.

Romantic Comedy

Romantic comedies are lighthearted plays that deal with the follies of young lovers or the misunderstandings between them. Shakespeare is closely associated with the romantic comedy, and his plays *A Midsummer Night's Dream* (circa 1596), *As You Like It* (circa 1600), and *Twelfth Night* (circa 1602) are examples of this form.

Features of a romantic comedy

- Romantic comedy features young lovers who are kept apart by some obstacles to their union. These obstacles may be brought about by parents and guardians, or could be the result of unique circumstances.
- The course of the love affair is not smooth. However, the couple eventually overcome all obstacles and the play ends happily (usually in marriage).
- Stock characters, such as the witty fool, the drunk, the beautiful heroine, the clever servant, etc., regularly appear in romantic comedies.
- There is sometimes a movement away from the everyday world to an unfamiliar location, or to a forest which is removed from the problems of the civilised world (for example, the forest outside Athens in *A Midsummer Night's Dream*, the forest of Arden in *As You Like It*, and the land of Illyria in *Twelfth Night*).
- The heroine is beautiful, witty, resourceful, and is sometimes forced by circumstances to disguise herself as a man (for example, Rosalind in *As You Like It* and Viola in *Twelfth Night*).
- Cross-dressing and mistaken identities are common plot elements in these plays. These plays also feature wordplay, puns and bawdy jokes.

With the coming of cinema, the romantic comedy form was successfully adapted for the screen and remains a very popular genre in film.

Tragicomedy

As the word implies, tragicomedy is tragedy and comedy mingled harmoniously together. It is distinct from tragedy that has comic scenes, and from comedies that include tragic episodes. The function of the porter's scene in *Macbeth* and the gravedigger's scene in *Hamlet* is not to evoke pure laughter, but to add to the intensity of the tragic tone of the plays. Similarly, the tragic background in a comedy such as *As You Like It* only makes us happy that all the wrongs done to the chief characters have been righted at the end. The tragicomedy, on the other hand, is an entirely individual form with its own set of features.

Features of a tragicomedy

- A tragicomedy blends the plot elements, character types, and subject matter of tragedy and comedy. Such a blend provides the audience with both a comic and a tragic view of life.
- The protagonist of a tragicomedy is usually under the threat of some impending disaster, but this danger is suddenly averted and the play ends happily.
- There is a mingling of upper and lower class characters in a tragicomedy—a feature that was strictly avoided by purists of classical forms.
- The characters often undergo some form of transformation before the play closes.

Notable examples of tragicomedy are William Shakespeare's *The Merchant of Venice* (circa 1597) and *The Winter's Tale* (circa 1611), and Francis Beaumont and John Fletcher's *Philaster* (circa 1610).

Chronicle Plays

After the defeat of the Spanish Armada in 1588, English nationalistic feelings were very high. This resulted in a revisiting of history by dramatists. English playwrights turned to Raphael Holinshed's *Chronicles of England*, first published in 1577, for their material. The term chronicle play is often used to describe plays dealing with historical facts, rather than with legends, myths, or fictitious events. Such plays are also known as **history plays**. Examples of chronicle plays include Christopher Marlowe's *Edward II* (1593) and William Shakespeare's *Richard III* (circa 1591) and *Henry V* (circa 1599).

Features of a chronicle play

- The subject of the play is the life of a king or a national hero.
- The play may feature both real historical characters (usually the major characters in the main plot) and invented characters (usually minor characters in the subplot, or composites of various historical characters).
- Although minor episodes were invented by the dramatist for dramatic or thematic purposes, the playwrights usually stuck to history with regard to more important events. Sometimes, historical events were telescoped to suit the narrative.
- Common themes and storylines include ambition, responsibility, succession to the throne, power and morality, and civil war.

Features of Elizabethan theatre and drama

Similar to the manner in which the peculiar features of Greek theatre affected the style and presentation of Greek plays, so too did Elizabethan theatre, with its own unique qualities, shape the drama of its time.

IMAGE C: The Globe theatre, where most of Shakespeare's plays were staged.

- The typical Elizabethan theatre house consisted of a large unroofed area called the 'yard'. This was enclosed by a three-storied, gallery type structure, which was usually round, square or octagonal in shape.
- The stage was an elevated platform that projected into the yard. This was divided into three parts—the front stage, the back stage and the upper stage. The front stage was used for depicting open spaces (such as a street scene). The back stage, with probably a few pieces of furniture, would represent a room in a palace or any other interior space. The upper stage was used for enacting a scene on the battlements or a balcony.

- There was no movable scenery. This proved to be both a blessing as well as a hurdle for the dramatist. Since there was no scenery depicting the setting, the playwright experienced limitless freedom as far as the setting of his plays was concerned. He could place his characters on stormy seas or in the dungeon of a castle. One scene could be set in Venice and the next in Belmont.
- The absence of a drop curtain posed certain difficulties. There was no way to let the audience know when a scene was completed. Dramatists usually overcame this hurdle by using a rhyming couplet to signal the end of a scene. The disposal of characters from the stage at the end of every scene had to be handled carefully. At the end of every scene, the characters gave instructions to each other as to where they should go or meet again, so that their exit from the stage did not appear awkward. When there was a death on the stage, actors would carry away the 'corpse' at the end of the scene.
- Women did not act on the stage. Acting was not considered a respectable profession, and it was considered immoral for a woman to perform in front of men. Female characters were played by young boys whose voices had not broken. The fact that boys played women in these plays allowed the dramatists opportunities for great dramatic irony, especially when female characters would disguise themselves as men.
- The main characters of Renaissance plays belonged to the upper class and the themes of these plays reflected their concerns—class mobility, wealth, war, religion, sex, and universal emotions such as love, hate, greed, ambition and jealousy.

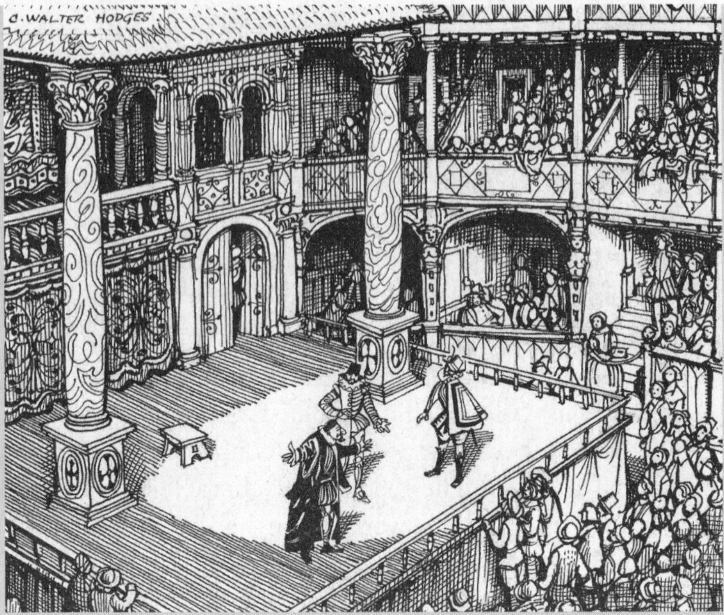

IMAGE D: An imaginative reconstruction of Shakespeare's Merchant of Venice being performed in an Elizabethan theatre. The groundlings watched from the 'pit', while those who could afford it sat in the gallery.

- Renaissance plays were, for the most part, written in blank verse. Prose lines were usually assigned only to commoners, servants, and other characters of low social status.
- All plays were performed during the day (usually at noon). Since the stage was exposed to daylight, night was indicated using simple props (such as torches) or dialogue.
- With regard to the audience, most commoners stood surrounding the front and sides of the stage, while the nobility (or those who could afford it) sat in reserved seats in the gallery. The audience mostly comprised uneducated folk who would boo and respond loudly to show approval or displeasure.

- Playscripts usually had no stage directions, and actors freely improvised, changing their performance—and even the dramatist's lines—based on immediate audience reaction.
- Renaissance acting companies had multiple plays in their repertory. Each day a different play was performed. Plays ran on the stage in a cyclical manner, sometimes for months on end.

Masque

The masque was a form of courtly dramatic entertainment that flourished in Europe in the sixteenth and seventeenth centuries. It originated in Italy and was very popular during the Stuart period.

Features of a masque

- The plot of a masque is slight, and is usually taken from mythology.
- The masque combined poetry, music, song and dance.
- It conveyed a moral message.
- The characters were ladies and gentlemen of the court. They wore elaborate masks while performing.
- Costly stage decor and extravagant costumes were produced for each play. The whole production was very spectacular.
- Masques were presented as a part of banquets or as a part of celebrations, such as a wedding, a coronation or a birthday. They were performed in courts or at the mansions of aristocrats.
- At the conclusion of a masque, the characters removed their masks and danced with partners from the audience.

Ben Jonson wrote some masques in the seventeenth century, featuring stage design by the famous architect Inigo Jones.

The best surviving example of a masque in English is Milton's *Comus* (1634).

Antimasque

Occasionally, the presentation of a masque was preceded by an antimasque. An antimasque was an allegory in song and dance, and involved fantastic and comic characters. The antimasque presented an episode of buffoonery or a grotesque dance, performed by professional actors. It served as a contrast to the masque and was often farcical. This was followed by the masque proper (performed by members of the court), which depicted the triumph of good over evil, and the restoration of order and harmony.

Comedy of Humours

The comedy of humours focused on certain characters with very distinct personality traits. This type of comedy, popular in the late sixteenth and the early seventeenth centuries, was based on the medieval theory of humours.

According to this theory, the body was believed to have been made up of four primary fluids or 'humours'—blood, yellow bile, black bile, and phlegm. The combination of these fluids determined a man's physical state and his character type. An imbalance of any one or the other fluids was thought to produce a distinct kind of disposition, as shown below.

Fluid	Personality type	Character traits
blood	sanguine	kindly, joyful, amorous
yellow bile	choleric	impatient, short-tempered
black bile	melancholic	brooding, affected, satiric
phlegm	phlegmatic	cowardly, obstinate, vengeful

Features of a comedy of humours

- This genre was developed primarily by Ben Jonson (1572–1637).
- The major characters in these plays, instead of being well-balanced individuals, are depicted as possessing a predominant humour that makes them appear distorted and eccentric.
- The names of the characters reveal their typical nature; for example, Wellbred, Knowall and Brainworm.
- The comedy of humours greatly influenced the later Restoration comedy of manners (see page 60).

Examples of this genre include Ben Jonson's *Every Man in His Humour* (1598), *Every Man out of His Humour* (1599) and *Volpone* (1606).

Heroic Tragedy

Heroic tragedy, written mostly during the Restoration period, aspired to epic splendour. It was influenced by the French neoclassical drama of Corneille. Sir William Davenant (circa 1606–68) helped to establish this type of drama in England. John Dryden (1631–1700) is considered the best exponent of this form.

Features of a heroic tragedy

- The subject of a heroic tragedy is the conflict between love and honour/duty. The events depicted (such as war) affect an entire nation. The theme is thus on an epic or heroic magnitude.
- Heroic tragedy is usually set in exotic, faraway lands, such as Mexico or India.
- The hero of this type of tragedy is depicted as a man of great strength or moral character. The heroine possesses unmatched beauty and unattainable virtues. These

characters are often caught in a situation in which they have to choose between their passionate love and their duty towards their country or family.

- The language is declamatory, bombastic and artificial.
- These tragedies are usually written in closed rhyming pairs of iambic pentameter lines. Due to its association with heroic tragedy, this verse form has come to be known as **heroic verse** or **heroic couplets**.

Examples of heroic tragedy include Dryden's *The Conquest of Granada* (1670) and *Love Triumphant* (1694). His *All for Love* (1677) is the best example of a heroic tragedy, although he did not use heroic couplets in it. The conventions of heroic drama were satirised in the play *The Rehearsal* (1671) by George Villiers, the Duke of Buckingham.

Comedy of Manners

This type of comedy was very popular during the Restoration period. After eleven years of strict Puritanical rule, with the theatres being closed and little other entertainment, the Restoration brought with it a wave of amoral behaviour and an excess of enjoyment. This newfound freedom is accurately reflected in the comedy of manners.

The earliest examples of the form may be seen in the plays of the ancient Greek playwright Menander, and later in the comedies of the Roman playwrights Plautus and Terence. Ben Jonson's comedy of humours and the plays of the French playwright Molière (such as *Tartuffe*, 1664, and *The Misanthrope*, 1666) were major influences on the genre.

Features of a comedy of manners

- It has as its theme the relations and intrigues of upper middle class ladies and gentlemen.

- The comedy of manners is known for its sparkling wit and repartee. **Repartee** is the quick give and take of witty dialogue that is sometimes mildly insulting.
- The characters are usually stock types such as charming rakes, jealous husbands, flirtatious women and foppish dandies.
- Since these plays reflected the immoral behaviour of the upper class, there was a lot of obscenity and licentiousness.
- The plots are elaborate and artificial, and the scenes are loosely constructed.
- There is usually a bedroom scene, with one or more characters hiding behind curtains or screens in order to eavesdrop on other characters.

The best examples of the comedy of manners from the Restoration period are William Wycherley's *The Country Wife* (1675) and William Congreve's *The Way of the World* (1700). The form continued to be popular in later years as evidenced by the popularity of such plays as Oliver Goldsmith's *She Stoops to Conquer* (1773), Richard Sheridan's *The School for Scandal* (1777), and Oscar Wilde's *The Importance of Being Earnest* (1895).

Genteel Comedy

The genteel comedy was a subgenre of the comedy of manners which developed in the middle of the eighteenth century. The term was first popularised by the English essayist and playwright Joseph Addison (1672–1719), who used it to describe comedies that portray the most artificial style of eighteenth-century drama. The best example of genteel comedy is Colley Cibber's *The Careless Husband* (1704).

Features of genteel comedy

- Genteel comedies faithfully reproduced the affectations of the upper class who lived during and after the reign of Queen Anne.
- Compared with the comedy of manners, the moral tone here is higher. Most of the indecencies of the earlier type of comedy are absent here.
- Genteel comedy is characterised by artificiality and sentimentality.
- The brilliant wit that was characteristic of the comedy of manners is missing in genteel comedy. The laughter arises out of the affectations of an artificial society, and not out of verbal fencing.

Sentimental Comedy

This type of comedy was a reaction to the comedy of manners (see page 60) and was popular in the mid-eighteenth century. The aim of sentimental comedy was to depict upon the stage ordinary men and women overwhelmed by misfortune and caught up in distressful situations, but ultimately triumphing over them. Although this type of comedy continued well into the nineteenth century, it began to decline in popularity from the last quarter of the eighteenth century.

Features of sentimental comedy

- Sentimental comedy is seemingly opposed to the spirit of true comedy, as they present a bleak view of life. There is no humour and the characters are shown to be suffering throughout the play. Only the contrived happy ending justifies calling it a comedy.
- The plays are extremely didactic and rely heavily upon the concept of poetic justice.

- They reflect the virtues of private life, rather than its vices.
- The hero is portrayed as being highly magnanimous and good-natured. The heroine is virtuous and pitiable, and the servants are honest.
- The distresses of the middle class are highlighted in order to evoke the sympathy of the audience.
- There is no wit or brilliance in these comedies.
- The dramatist's aim was to impart a moral to make up for the amorality of the comedy of manners.

The best examples of sentimental comedies are Colley Cibber's *Love's Last Shift* (1696), George Farquhar's *The Constant Couple* (1699), and Richard Steele's *The Conscious Lovers* (1722).

Domestic Tragedy

Domestic tragedy is a play about middle or lower class people and their problems. George Lillo's *The London Merchant* (1731) and the German poet Christian Friedrich Hebbel's *Maria Magdalena* (1844) are examples of domestic tragedies. The term is also used to describe the plays of the Norwegian playwright Henrik Ibsen and some modern playwrights.

Features of a domestic tragedy

- The play is serious and generally realistic in style.
- The subject matter is drawn from the concerns of middle or lower class society. The action revolves around personal or domestic matters, rather than matters of state or national importance.
- The characters are common people with whom the audience is able to easily identify.
- They arouse pity and sympathy, rather than the sublime effect of grand tragedy.

- The domestic tragedies of the eighteenth century and later were written mostly in prose.

Closet Drama

Closet drama is a play which is not intended to be staged in a theatre; it is meant only for private reading. John Milton's *Samson Agonistes* (1671) and Percy Bysshe Shelley's *Prometheus Unbound* (1820) are notable examples. Johann Wolfgang von Goethe's *Faust, Part I* (1808) and *Faust, Part II* (1832) were originally closet dramas, but are now being performed on the stage. Many closet dramas were written in the Victorian Age.

Features of closet drama

- The popularity of closet drama among writers in Western Europe in the 1800s may be seen as a reaction to the decline of verse tragedy in the nineteenth century. Audiences were more interested in melodrama and comedy. Since the staging of plays in verse was becoming commercially unprofitable, dramatists had to content themselves with reaching out to readers instead of an audience.
- Since these plays are designed especially for reading, they do not concern themselves with stage technique.
- These plays usually have little action, and feature long, philosophical passages.
- Closet drama was often composed in verse, inspired by classical models.

Farce

Farce is a type of low comedy intended to provoke laughter. It is associated with burlesque, clowning and buffoonery. Farce has no other intention other than entertainment and a good-natured depiction of folly. Unlike satire, it does not aim at correcting or criticising society.

One could trace the origin of farce to the ancient Greek comedian Aristophanes. The Latin term *farsa* (derived from *farcire*, meaning 'to stuff') was first used to refer to passages of medieval French that were inserted in the Latin text of the Mass. Later, it was used to describe the insertions to religious plays in England—more popularly known as interludes (see page 49). It is from this use that the modern meaning of farce has developed. As a separate form of entertainment, it came into vogue towards the close of the seventeenth century.

Features of a farce

- Farce is lowbrow comedy.
- There is exaggerated physical action and slapstick.
- The characters are exaggerated types, rather than being true to life.
- It is full of absurd situations and improbable (even nonsensical) actions.
- There are several surprises and disclosures in a farce.
- Character and dialogue are subservient to plot and situation.
- The plot is complex and intricate.

The best example of a farce is the English playwright Brandon Thomas's *Charley's Aunt* (1892). There are strong farcical elements in William Shakespeare's *A Midsummer Night's Dream* (circa 1596) and *The Merry Wives of Windsor* (circa 1597). Farces were also used in tragedies for comic relief—for example, in Christopher Marlowe's *Dr Faustus* (circa 1592).

Melodrama

Just as farce is exaggerated comedy, melodrama is exaggerated tragedy. Originally, the term was applied to all musical plays, including operas. In the early part of the nineteenth century, popular theatres in London put up plays that were accompanied by music. In modern usage, the term is used to describe any kind of writing that relies heavily upon sensationalism and improbable events.

Features of a melodrama

- A melodrama has sensational themes and plots full of intrigue.
- The characters are flat (see page 104)—perfect heroes, virtuous maidens, dastardly villains, helpless aged parents, faithful servants, and other stereotypical characters. Good and evil characters are easily distinguishable.
- The action may be violent and bloody. The plots feature murders, abductions, drowning, fires, etc.
- The language is overwrought and full of heightened emotion. Intense emotions and exaggerated gestures were common in melodrama.
- The protagonists suffer or are endangered due to the machinations of the antagonists; however, they triumph in the end thanks to their endurance and virtue (or due to pure luck).
- Very often, novels were adapted for the stage in the form of melodrama.

Examples of melodrama include *The Red Rover* (1829) by Edward Fitzball; *The Streets of London* (1864) by Dion Boucicault; and dramatisations of sensational stories, such as those of Sweeney Todd, 'the Demon Barber of Fleet Street'.

Cup-and-Saucer Drama

This name was given to a type of drama, popular in the nineteenth century, which focused on realistic, domestic actions of the upper class. Since the action was often set in the drawing room of a house and the script included the serving of tea, these plays were referred to as cup-and-saucer drama. The English dramatist Thomas William Robertson's plays *Society* (1865) and *Caste* (1867) are examples of this genre.

Features of cup-and-saucer drama

- These plays often tackled serious contemporary issues such as class and social prejudices.
- The style of presentation was naturalistic. Stage settings and props were made as realistic as possible.
- There are no exaggerated, declamatory speeches. The characters behaved like ordinary people in real-life situations.

Problem Play

The problem play, also known as a **comedy of ideas**, is one in which the problems of society are presented with an unconventional slant. This genre developed in the nineteenth century in France. It was perfected by the Norwegian dramatist Henrik Ibsen (1828–1906), whose play *The Doll's House* (1879), highlighting the lack of social opportunities for women, is an outstanding example of the form. Inspired by Ibsen, the English playwright George Bernard Shaw (1856–1950) wrote many problem plays, such as *Mrs Warren's Profession* (1893), which talks about prostitution. Other problem plays include Ibsen's *Ghosts* (1882) and *An Enemy of the People* (1882), Harley Granville-Barker's *The Voysey Inheritance* (1905), and John Galsworthy's *Strife* (1909).

Features of a problem play

- The problem play deals with contemporary social issues.
- The theatre is used by the dramatist as a forum for social, political and moral discussions. The playwright's aim is to sensitise the audience towards the issues depicted.

- The characters in the play typically represent conflicting points of view.
- The dramatist often exhibits his own point of view through one or more of the characters.
- The mode of presentation is realistic.
- A variation of the problem play is the **discussion play**. Instead of incorporating the theme into the plot, the playwright makes his characters discuss the social issue on stage in the form of extended debates. An example is Shaw's *Misalliance* (1910).

Well-made Play

The term 'well-made play' is used to describe a play based on a fixed formula of a complex and highly artificial plot, and an ending in which all the problems are neatly resolved and everyone is happy. It was made popular in the 1820s by the French playwright Eugène Scribe (1791–1861), who wrote many plays using this formula. Victorien Sardou (1831–1908) was another French dramatist who specialised in writing such plays. In England, Wilkie Collins wrote plays that could be classified under this category.

Features of a well-made play

- The well-made play is very tightly plotted. A large and essential portion of the story, told through exposition, has usually taken place in the past, before the action of the play. The on-stage action consists of a series of complications that are the natural result of the backstory.
- The dramatist usually places the climax of the action as close to the end of the play as possible.
- The plot often turns on a secret that is revealed to the audience, but which most of the characters in the play are not aware of.

- Such plays often featured suffering protagonists, romantic conflicts, suspense arising due to misunderstandings between characters, mistaken identities, and secret information.
- A characteristic feature of the well-made play is that of important papers or letters falling into wrong hands. Such documents are also used to bring about a twist in the plot.
- The revelation of the hitherto unknown secret causes a reversal of fortune.

Later playwrights such as Émile Zola and George Bernard Shaw denounced the artificial mode of the well-made play, and the term began to be used mostly in a derogatory manner. Although he criticised the conventions of the well-made play, Shaw often used its techniques in several of his plays. Other playwrights too adapted the techniques of the well-made play to suit their dramatic purpose, for example, Henrik Ibsen in *A Doll's House* (1879) and Oscar Wilde in *The Importance of Being Earnest* (1895).

Expressionist Drama

Expressionism was an early twentieth-century art movement in which inner experiences were emphasised and subjectively expressed through a distorted rendition of reality. Expressionist playwrights were strongly influenced by the dramatic forms and stage techniques popularised by the Swedish dramatist August Strindberg (1849–1912). Expressionist drama began in Germany and spread across Europe, and later to the USA.

Features of expressionist drama

- The mode of presentation is non-realistic.
- Characters in these plays are one-sided, often representing a single idea or attitude.

- The characters are placed in situations in which the objects of the outer world are distorted in order to reflect the tortured minds of the characters or the dramatist. The expressionists believed that the human spirit was the real shaper of reality and that the surface appearance was important only because it was a reflection of the inner vision. Expressionist drama thus made use of distorted sets, lighting, and costumes to portray disturbed psyches.
- The speeches are short and jerky, and the movements, machine-like.

Strindberg's *A Dream Play* (1901), *To Damascus* (1898–1904), and *The Ghost Sonata* (1907) pioneered the form. In these plays, time and place shift freely. Characters multiply and merge. Objects change their appearances frequently. The genre found full expression in such German plays as Oskar Kokoschka's *Murderer, the Hope of Women* (1909) and Walter Hasenclever's *The Son* (1914), and in the American plays *The Hairy Ape* (1922) by Eugene O'Neill and *The Adding Machine* (1923) by Elmer Rice.

Epic Theatre

Epic theatre developed in Germany in the 1920s. This type of drama was founded by the German theatre director Erwin Piscator (1893–1966) and popularised by the German dramatist Bertolt Brecht (1898–1956). Brecht used the name 'epic' to distinguish his mode of writing from the traditional 'dramatic' theatre. Later in his career, Brecht preferred the label **dialectical theatre** to refer to the kind of plays he produced.

Features of epic theatre

- This type of drama was devoted to the expression of political ideas and ideals.

- Epic theatre was a reaction against contemporary forms of theatre such as the well-made play (see page 68), with its neat and manipulative plots, and melodrama (see page 65), with its extreme and insincere emotions. Epic theatre also reacted against surrealism and the Theatre of Cruelty (see below).
- Brecht was also critical of the naturalistic approach of the Russian actor and theatre director Constantin Stanislavski (1863–1938), in which the latter tried to absorb the audience completely into the fictional world of the drama through a realistic and natural portrayal of life. Brecht believed that this would result in a form of escapism. He wanted his audience to be fully present in the moment.
- One of the chief aims of epic theatre is to make sure that the audience is always conscious of the fact that they are watching a play, so that they could reflect on the action critically. Brecht developed what he called the 'alienation effect', which created a sense of detachment in the audience from the action of the play. Unlike traditional drama, epic theatre does not wish its audience to empathise with the characters. In order to achieve this, Brecht used tactics such as flooding the entire theatre with bright lights, 'breaking the fourth wall' by making his characters directly address the audience, and making the actors move the sets in full view of the audience.
- Notable features of such plays include a chorus-like narrator, slide projection, music, and placards.

Examples of epic theatre include Brecht's *The Threepenny Opera* (1928) and *Mother Courage and her Children* (1939).

Theatre of Cruelty

The term 'Theatre of Cruelty' was coined by the French poet and playwright Antonin Artaud (1896–1948). According to his theory of drama, a play should shock the audience in order to release subconscious and hidden truths.

Features of the Theatre of Cruelty

- Artaud wanted to do away with the stage, sets and props.
- He envisioned actors as performing all around an audience.
- This type of theatre included vivid lighting effects, mime, and sensational (even horrific) action.
- Artaud's ideas greatly influenced important avant-garde playwrights such as Jean Genet (1910–86), Jerzy Grotowski (1933–99), and Peter Brook (born 1925).

In 1935, Artaud produced an adaptation of Percy Bysshe Shelley's play *The Cenci,* based on his principles of the Theatre of Cruelty. A more prominent example of this type of drama is the German playwright Peter Weiss's *Marat/Sade* (1963).

Artaud's theories have been influential in creating an offshoot of modern drama known as 'a **happening**'. A happening could be defined as any action (or actions) which affects the senses—sight, sound, smell or touch. It need not necessarily be performed on the stage. It could be enacted in any public place such as a street, a circus ring or the market place. The audience could even participate in the action if they so desire.

Absurd Drama

The Theatre of the Absurd emerged in France during the 1950s and is an important movement in twentieth-century drama. This type of drama is based on twentieth-century ideas like **existentialism**, which looked upon man as an isolated creature in a world that had no inherent value or meaning. The human condition is seen as an absurd and meaningless one that is full of angst.

The term 'Absurd drama' is applied to the work of certain dramatists who were active in the 1950s, including Samuel Beckett (1906–89), Arthur Adamov (1908–70), Eugène Ionesco (1909–94), Jean Genet (1910–86), and Harold Pinter (1930–2008). The term was coined by the English critic Martin Esslin in the essay 'Theatre of the Absurd' (1960).

These plays reject the traditional elements of drama, such as a linear plot, realistic dialogue, and a recognisable setting. As Esslin pointed out, Absurd drama expects the viewer to 'draw his own conclusions, make his own errors'. Beckett's *Waiting for Godot* (1953) presents two tramps in a wasteland, waiting in vain for an unidentified person, Godot, whose very existence is questioned by them every now and then.

Features of Absurd drama

- Absurd drama represents the disorientation of living in an unfriendly and hostile universe.
- It is a theatre of situation as against a theatre of sequential events.
- The action in an absurd drama does not tell a story, but presents a pattern of images designed to reflect the perplexity of man's existence in an incomprehensible world.
- There is no plot or story in the traditional sense in such plays. They lack formal logic and conventional structure.
- The plays often depict the emptiness and nothingness of life. For example, Beckett's *Waiting for Godot* revolves around the nonappearance of a character named Godot. In Ionesco's *The Chairs* (1952), an 'Old Man' and an 'Old Woman', apparently the last two human beings on earth, arrange chairs to seat 'everyone'. They are expecting a speaker, who turns out to be a deaf-mute. Ionesco notes that, 'The last decisive moment of the play should be the expression of ... absence.' At times the plot may focus

on some inexplicable metamorphosis or inconceivable happening. For example, in Ionesco's *Amédée, or How to Get Rid of It* (1954), a playwright and his wife are faced with the problem of trying to get rid of a steadily growing corpse.

- The characters are depicted as being aimless and lost in a world that is beyond their comprehension. They are incapable of rational thought and action and are often portrayed as automatons who can speak only in clichés. They are usually flat characters.
- Sometimes the characters are depicted as being terrorised by some external force or person. For instance, in Pinter's *The Birthday Party* (1957), Stanley is intimidated by Goldberg and McCann. In some Absurd plays, characters are shown against the backdrop of a world threatened by science. An excellent example of this is Ionesco's *Rhinoceros* (1959), in which Berenger finds himself the only surviving human being in a world full of rhinoceroses.
- The dialogue is pointless and at times funny. Absurdists revel in making use of technological jargon, clichés, triteness and baby talk. Mere prattle is employed to reveal the futility of communication. Dramatists like Pinter often use ellipses or dashes for important parts of dialogue. See, for instance, these lines from his play *The Caretaker* (1960)—

  Aston: More or less exactly what you …
  Davies: You see, what I mean to say … what I'm getting at is … I mean, what sort of jobs … *(Pause)*
  Aston: Well, there's things like the stairs … and the ... the bells …
  Davies: But it'd be a matter … wouldn't it … it'd be a matter of a broom … isn't it?
- Slapstick is often a part of absurd drama.

Kitchen Sink Drama

This was a term applied to certain British plays of the 1950s and 1960s which focused on the lives of working class protagonists in a realistic manner. Kitchen sink drama was associated with the **Angry Young Men** movement in English literature.

In the 1950s, a group of British novelists and dramatists from middle class and working class backgrounds became known for their anti-establishment works. Their plays and novels expressed great dissatisfaction with the socioeconomic and political conditions of the time, and gave vent to the disillusionment and discontent they felt at the failure of the welfare state to live up to its promises. The mood of anger and frustration in their works led to them being labelled 'Angry Young Men'. The plays of the dramatists in this group were referred to as 'kitchen sink drama', the term being a reference to the increasing interest among contemporary artists in themes centred around domestic scenes.

Features of kitchen sink drama

- Kitchen sink drama portrays the lives of the ordinary, educated, lower class youth, who often worked unsatisfying menial jobs and lived in cramped homes.
- The characters are often from poor, industrial parts of the country, and the dialogue reflects the colloquial language of these regions.
- The protagonist is typically an intelligent young man from the lower-middle or working class (quite like most of the 'Angry Young Men' writers), who rails at the established social order.
- These plays attack the stifling traditions and attitudes of the rigid class system of their time.
- Kitchen sink drama, with its focus on a realistic portrayal of working class life, could be seen as a reaction to the

well-made play (see page 68), which was known for its artificiality, and also as a reaction against the working-class stereotypes portrayed in plays by upper-middle class writers.

John Osborne's *Look Back in Anger* (1956) is a classic example of this type of drama. It represents a whole generation's resentment against the establishment. Jimmy Porter, the antihero of the play, is the prototype of the 'angry young man'. Other plays in this mode include *The Hamlet of Stepney Green* (1957) by Bernard Kops and *Chicken Soup with Barley* (1958) by Arnold Wesker.

Poor Theatre

This was also known as Laboratory Theatre and is associated with the Polish theatre director Jerzy Grotowski (1933–99). He referred to his style of theatre as 'poor' since he avoided the usual trappings and expensive technology of regular ('rich') theatre. It is experimental and noncommercial in nature.

Features of poor theatre

- Poor Theatre can be performed in any bare space. It does not require a traditional stage.
- This form of theatre depends heavily on the actor's voice, body movement, and skill.
- The actors perform in and around the audience. The space between the performers and the audience is reduced to allow maximum communication between the two.
- Minimal props are used. The lights are stationary. The costumes are plain. Vocal effects are often used in place of instrumental music.

Poor theatre proved to be very influential in art theatre and in alternative theatre. Grotowski's ideas paved the way for **third theatre**. This involved street plays which were performed without much emphasis on lighting, costumes or make-up. The formal bindings of the proscenium theatre were given up. The Indian dramatist Badal Sircar's plays, such as *Bhoma* and *Stale News*, were written and performed according to the principles of third theatre.

Bread and Puppet Theatre

'Bread and puppet theatre' is a form of puppet theatre founded by Peter Schumann (born 1934) in 1963 in New York. It is currently based in Vermont, in northeastern United States.

Features of bread and puppet theatre

- Bread and puppet theatre is a form of politically radical activist theatre.
- It features enormous puppets (somtimes ten to fifteen feet tall).
- It owes its name to the practice of sharing bread (with a certain dipping sauce) with the audience. This was done in order to create a sense of community and also to establish the fact that art was as basic to life as bread.
- Bread and puppet theatre has played a politically active part in many demonstrations since the 1960s, and is especially remembered for its anti-war protests during the Vietnam War (1955–75).

Its performances are common during parades, including Fourth of July celebrations (during which tall effigies of Uncle Sam on stilts may be seen). Two notable shows of this troupe include *Nativity 1992* and *The Divine Reality Comedy*.

One-act Play

The one act play is a dramatic performance that has only one act. The one act play is to drama what the short story is to the novel. One may trace its antecedents to the religious plays of medieval England (see page 48). Mystery plays, miracle plays, morality plays, and interludes were all short plays dealing with a single theme. With the passage of time, these plays gave way to the more elaborate five-act play. It reappeared as the after-piece that was popular with eighteenth-century audiences. The close of the nineteenth century, which saw an upsurge in experimental theatre, witnessed the growth of this genre. The one-act play was often used as a curtain-raiser, before the commencement of the main play. Nowadays, the form has become popular in its own right.

Features of a one-act play

- It has only one act. It may or may not be divided into short scenes.
- It has all the elements that are found in full-length drama—plot, dialogue, characters and setting—but it focuses only upon a single episode or situation.
- The subject matter of a one act play may vary from the serious to the comic.
- The number of characters is usually limited.
- Like the longer play, the one-act play also has an exposition and rising action. However, the dramatist is forced to be economical in his delineation of characters and in the development of the plot. The climax often forms the conclusion of the play.
- Like the short story, the one act play also thrives on a twist or surprise ending. For example, in Stanley Houghton's *The Dear Departed* (1908), as the daughters fight over the possessions of their 'dead' father, the father himself appears on the scene and announces that he plans to marry.

Some well-known one-act plays include Anton Chekhov's *A Marriage Proposal* (1890) and Samuel Beckett's *Krapp's Last Tape* (1958). One should not underestimate the one-act play as being less profound in comparison to full-length drama. In the hands of a good dramatist, this form is capable of great complexity; for example, W.B. Yeats's *The Pot of Broth* (1902) and J.M. Synge's *Riders to the Sea* (1904).

Types of Theatre Spaces

Proscenium theatre

In a proscenium theatre, the stage is located at one end of the auditorium, and is separated from the rest of the auditorium by a proscenium arch. The audience is seated facing the stage. The proscenium arch acts as a 'picture frame' through which the audience can view the action on the stage. The actors perform facing the audience, who are able to see only one side of the scene being performed (as though through an invisible fourth wall of the room in the scene). The actors need to focus

Image E: A proscenium theatre

only in one direction, and the scenery too needs only be one-dimensional or two-dimensional as the audience can have only a frontal view.

This type of theatre was very popular for staging plays in the nineteenth and early twentieth centuries. In modern theatre, actors 'break the proscenium' (or 'break the fourth wall') when they directly address the audience or when they walk out of the stage and mingle with the audience.

THEATRE IN THE ROUND

Theatre in the round, also known as an **arena theatre** or an **island stage**, is a type of theatre arranged so as to allow the audience to surround the actors on all sides. Actors enter and exit from different directions through gaps in the seating arrangement. The stage is usually on an even level with the seats, or lowered below the audience in a 'pit' or 'arena'. Such a configuration removes the fourth wall: the actor and the audience share the same space.

It is probable that mystery and miracle plays were performed in a similar stage configuration. It was much later that the central stage gave way to the thrust stage of Elizabethan times (see IMAGE D on page 56) and the later proscenium stage. This

IMAGE F: A theatre in the round stage configuration. The audience surrounds the stage on all four sides.

type of theatre was not uncommon in the experimental theatre of the twentieth century.

THRUST STAGE

This is a type of stage that projects out and extends into the audience, which surrounds it on three sides. There may or may not be a proscenium arch in the backstage area. Many modern dramatists prefer the thrust stage, though directors need to ensure that actors, props and scenery do not block the view of any member of the audience.

IMAGE G: A thrust stage. The audience surrounds the stage on three sides.

SITE-SPECIFIC THEATRE

This refers to the production of plays in an unconventional location that was not originally conceived for staging plays; for example, a hotel or a park. This type of theatre makes use of the site's unique features, is flexible, and is more interactive than conventional theatre.

Environmental theatre refers to situating a play in an environment similar to the one in which the play is set; for example, performing *Hamlet* in a Danish castle.

In **promenade theatre**, the audience watches the action happening among them as they stand or move about (instead of sitting). They can even follow the performers around the performance space.

Black box theatre

This is a more recent innovation in theatre. It consists of a huge, empty, rectangular room (often with plain black walls). There is no fixed seating and all furniture (like chairs for the audience) is movable and optional.

3

Prose: Nonfiction

Prose is one of the two major forms of literary expression, the other being poetry. If asked to distinguish between prose and poetry, one could say prose is like walking, that is to say, it is functional, while poetry is like dancing, which is decorative or ornamental. Prose is the medium that is regularly used in spoken language, letters, articles, newspapers and short stories. The word 'prose' is derived from the Latin 'prosa', meaning 'straightforward'. It is thus a direct and plain form of language that is used in everyday communication.

There are several artistic manifestations of prose too. Generally, a prose writer does not make use of rhyme and metre, which are the chief characteristics of poetry. This is not to say that prose cannot be artistic and pleasing. A skilful writer makes use of several devices like puns, paradox, alliteration and metaphors to adorn her/his work.

There is no prescribed style for writing prose. There are as many styles as there are writers, and these may range from the most simple to the very complex. Francis Bacon, one of the early exponents of this form in modern English, preferred to write in simple, short sentences. John Milton, on the other hand, wrote extremely long and complicated sentences that were Latinate in style. In the twentieth century, people preferred a fast-paced and lucid style which avoided the use of bombastic and high-sounding words.

Since the term 'prose' is used to cover a vast variety of writing, from the ordinary, personal letter to the highly artistic novel, it may be studied under different headings such as nonfiction, fiction and literary criticism. There are several forms of nonfiction prose writing. We will examine three chief forms in this section—

Biography
Autobiography
Essay

The two other major categories of prose writing—fiction and literary criticism—will be examined in the following sections.

Biography

A biography is an account of a person's life written by someone else. The word 'biography' comes from the Greek words 'bios', meaning 'life', and 'graphein', meaning 'to write'. As a genre, it rose in prominence from the second half of the seventeenth century. It differs from history in that it is a record of one individual. Two definite events are included in almost every biography—birth and death.

Origin and growth

There were very few biographies in the Early Middle Ages. The only works which came close to biography were **hagiographies**, or the lives of saints. These works idealised their subjects and followed a set style. Hagiographies were written not to describe the subject's career or personality, but to set before the readers examples of pious living.

In the Late Middle Ages, the biography became more secular, and books on the lives of kings, knights and soldiers began to appear. We can trace the origin of such biographies to Plutarch's *Lives*, in which he described the lives of twenty-three Greeks and twenty-three Romans in pairs. This work (written in the latter half of the first century) later became an important source of plots for dramatists like Shakespeare. Giovanni Boccaccio's *Life of Dante* (c. 1355) is another important work.

The most popular among these was *Morte d'Arthur* (1485) by Sir Thomas Malory. During the Elizabethan Age, there were several translations of classical biographies.

These works inspired the humanists of the Renaissance, who focused on secular subjects and wrote about artists and poets. Giorgio Vasari's *Lives of the Painters* (1550), William Roper's *Life of Sir Thomas More* (1626), and Thomas Cavendish's *Life of Cardinal Wolsey* (1641) are some of the important works that belong to this period. An influential biography of this age was Francis Bacon's *History of Henry VII* (1622), which was significant because of the way the author juxtaposed a psychological analysis of his subject against the historical context of his reign.

In the seventeenth century, the biography became popular. John Aubrey's *Brief Lives* belongs to this period, but was not published till 1813. He focused on the personal details of the subject's life and often failed to distinguish between fact and gossip. The word 'biography' was used for the first time by John Dryden who defined it as 'the history of particular men's lives'. At that stage, it did not have any particular form. It was just a loose collection of random incidents lacking the artistic principle of selection and arrangement.

In the eighteenth century, biography became an art form and authors used the tools of the novelist to make their work readable and interesting. Dr Samuel Johnson was one of the greatest biographers of this period and was also the subject of one of the most famous biographies ever written—*The Life of Samuel Johnson* (1791) by James Boswell. Boswell was an acquaintance of Johnson, and he combined his firsthand knowledge of his subject with the information he gathered from various other sources.

The biography underwent a change in the nineteenth century, in that it glossed over the unsavoury aspects of the subject's life in order to appear respectable. The prudishness and gentility of the Victorian Age was responsible for this change in approach.

'Debunking' is a modern trend in biography, in which the biographer ruthlessly dissects his subject. Lytton Strachey made this popular through his work *Eminent Victorians* (1918). In it, he exposed the shortcomings of his subjects in an irreverent manner.

Biographers today focus upon research and objectivity, and make use of their literary skills as prose writers. In the twentieth century, the biography remains a highly respectable form and a source of information.

Features of a biography

- A biography is the story of an individual; the focus is on this individual, and other characters, even if they are greater in some way, play only a subsidiary role.
- A good biography traces not only the achievements of the subject, but also highlights her/his personality and character.
- A biography is not a mere compilation of dry facts. A biographer takes care to arrange and present her/his material in a pleasing and artistic manner. A well-written biography brings the personality of the subject to life.

Problems faced by a biographer

- It is quite difficult for a biographer who has not lived constantly with her/his subject to give an accurate picture of the person. Some of the best biographies have been written by those who have known their subjects intimately. For example, Boswell was a very close friend of Samuel Johnson. Similarly, John Gibson Lockhart, who wrote a biography of Sir Walter Scott, was the latter's son-in-law and had firsthand knowledge of his subject.

- It is not possible for a biographer to always know his subject personally. In such cases, the task of gathering, sifting and presenting information about a person becomes very challenging. The biographer is forced to piece together the life of her/his subject from sources like records, letters and journals.
- Another difficulty in writing a biography is trying to compress the different facets of a life in all its complexity—physical, intellectual, psychological and moral. A person's life is composed of thoughts and feelings which she/he may have suppressed or left unexpressed, and the biographer can only guess at these.
- Great skill and discretion is to be exercised in selecting the events and incidents in the life of the subject. If too much importance is given to personal details, there exists the danger of slipping into mere gossip. At the same time, a biographer should give enough insight into the subject's personality to satisfy the reader's desire to know about the person.

In spite of all these obstacles, English literature has a rich collection of biographies.

Qualities of an ideal biographer

- An ideal biographer is generally expected to be detached from her/his subject and to reveal only a professional interest, while refraining from offering her/his own views or opinions. She/he is expected to be impartial in analysing the life of her/his subject, and objectively present both the vices and the virtues of the person.
- A biographer is expected to refrain from attributing a moral or any other utilitarian motive to his work. It is inadvisable to use the life of the subject to illustrate any theory that might be close to the biographer's heart.

- A biographer should guard against the temptation to exaggerate the virtues of her/his subject as it would result in a biased eulogy. This was a common feature of biographies written by the Victorians.

Autobiography

An autobiography is a kind of biography in which the author tells the story of his or her own life. The term is believed to have been first used in its present sense by Robert Southey in 1809. According to the American poet H.W. Longfellow, 'Autobiography is a product of firsthand experience; biography, of secondhand knowledge.'

Dr Johnson was of the firm opinion that no man was better qualified to write about his life than himself. This is debatable, as a person's memory could be unreliable. It is difficult for a person to accurately recall all the details of his or her early life, and one may be forced to depend on other people for information. Yet another issue is that one might share only those details that one wishes to. So, an autobiography becomes unreliable as a source of information since disagreeable facts could be misrepresented, glossed over, or completely ignored.

Origin and growth

The first autobiography of note is St Augustine's *Confessions*, written in the fourth century. Similar examples of autobiographical works may be found in classical and medieval literature, especially in the form of the **apology** (a formal written defence of one's life and work, or of something one believes in) and confessional writing. However, it was only after the sixteenth century that the autobiography as a form became popular. During the Renaissance, there was a growing interest in the human being, which resulted in people focusing on the exploration of character and personality. The growing trend of subjectivity proved to be the right climate for the development of the autobiography. *Grace Abounding to the Chief of Sinners* (1666) by John Bunyan is an early modern example of autobiographical writing. In the seventeenth century, maintaining journals and diaries became fashionable and this practice paved the way for compiling **memoirs** (an account of the author's personal experiences, memories and feelings). The French philosopher Jean-Jacques Rousseau's *Confessions* (1782–89) was an influential model for others attempting to write their own biographies. The next century witnessed the rise of the novel. Since then, there have been many novels with thinly disguised autobiographical protagonists and narratives, such as Charlotte Brontë's *Jane Eyre* (1847), Charles Dickens's *David Copperfield* (1850), and George Eliot's *The Mill on the Floss* (1860). An example of an autobiographical poem is Wordsworth's *The Prelude* (1850). In the nineteenth and twentieth centuries, several autobiographies were published. Some well-known autobiographies include *Up from Slavery* (1901) by Booker T. Washington, *The Story of My Life* (1903) by Helen Keller, and *I Know Why the Caged Bird Sings* (1969) by Maya Angelou. Today, we have autobiographies written by people from all walks of life—actors, sportsmen, politicians, social workers, doctors and spiritual gurus.

Features of an autobiography

- An autobiography is not a mere narration of events. It is a reflection of the author's inner life as well as her/his public achievements, set in the context of the time.
- An autobiography is made interesting to read by presenting details in an artistic and engaging manner while remaining truthful.

Problems faced by an autobiographer

- An autobiographer might set out to give the reader a truthful account of her/his life. However, it is not always easy to recapture accurately all the details of an event in one's past. It is almost impossible to recreate authentically all the impressions and emotions experienced in the distant past. Therefore one has to depend on the impressions and memories of others, especially to recreate incidents from one's childhood and early life.

- Another difficulty that an autobiographer faces is in the recounting of episodes that involve other people. Care has to be taken to avoid showing them in a bad light as that could cause embarrassment and ill will.
- Yet another difficulty is related to the artistic nature of an autobiography. Herbert Spencer, the nineteenth-century English philosopher, pointed out that the biography and the autobiography omitted details of daily life that are natural to all humans, and focused only on the exceptional and the extraordinary. This might lead the reader into believing that the subjects of such works led extraordinary lives.

Qualities of an ideal autobiographer

- While being as lively and engaging as possible, the author must guard against sounding pompous and boastful. One must also not stray into exaggeration and embellishment when writing about one's achievements.
- She/he should give due credit to those who played important roles in her/his life.

Biography and autobiography compared

What we look for in a biography is objectivity and factual accuracy. In an autobiography, we look for subjectivity: we want the writer to give us the little, personal details about her/his life. Compare, for example, D.G. Tendulkar's biography of M.K. Gandhi, *Mahatma* (1951), with Gandhi's autobiography *The Story of My Experiments with Truth* (1927). A good biography succeeds in giving us perspective. That is, we get an objective view of the background, history, and influences that had an impact upon the life of the subject (as in Tendulkar's biography). The advantage of an autobiography, on the other hand, is that we can learn about the motives, emotions, hopes, fears, doubts and joys that only the writer can know (as we do in Gandhi's autobiography).

Essay

An essay could be defined as a short piece of writing that reveals the writer's views or analysis of a particular subject. As a literary form, it is difficult to study systematically since it varies greatly in style, treatment and method. It could range in length from Francis Bacon's brief pieces of concentrated wisdom, running into a page or two, to the book-length pieces by John Locke, Lord Macaulay and Herbert Spencer. The essay could vary in subject matter too. For example, Bacon shared his views on various subjects ranging from love, death and atheism to travel, marriage and gardens. The essays of the French Renaissance philosopher Michel de Montaigne are an assortment of random thoughts, quotations and anecdotes. Even with regard to treatment, each writer has his or her own style in approaching the subject. Charles Lamb employed a conversational style, taking the reader through a gamut of emotions, while Jonathan Swift used biting satire to attack his opponents in his essays. So, a definition of the essay form cannot be made based upon its length, subject matter or treatment.

Some definitions of an essay

The word 'essay' has been applied to nearly every kind of writing except poems, plays and stories. For the sake of convenience, we could define the essay as a brief composition in prose on any particular subject or branch of a subject. According to Samuel Johnson, an essay is 'a loose sally of the mind; an irregular, undigested piece; not a regular and orderly composition'. 'A good essay', said E.V. Lucas, 'more than a novel, a poem, a play, or a treatise, is personality translated into print.' Aldous Huxley defined the essay as 'a literary device for saying almost everything about almost anything'.

Montaigne (1533–92) could be considered the father of the modern essay. It was he who first used the term 'essais', meaning 'attempt', 'experiment' or 'endeavour', for this type of writing (in 1580). His essays were informal in nature and had a warmth and grace about them. In 1597, Francis Bacon (following Montaigne) applied the word 'essay' to this genre for the first time in English. Bacon is considered to be a pioneer of this form.

Origin and growth of the essay

In Bacon's view, the letters of the Roman writers Cicero and Seneca could be considered essays rather than mere letters as these contained their thoughts on various matters. Plutarch, another classical writer, could also be seen as a forerunner of this form. The personal essay, however, owes its existence to Montaigne, who first used the word 'essai' to describe such writing.

Francis Bacon, who wrote several essays in English, followed a style of his own, favouring concentrated, business-like prose. This was very different from Montaigne's leisurely style and amused tone. Abraham Cowley, who wrote in the 1660s, followed the personal and informal style of Montaigne. Other writers who wrote in this form were Sir William Temple and John Dryden. Temple and Dryden were responsible for paving the way for the development of the essay in the seventeenth and eighteenth centuries. They had a great impact on the essayists Joseph Addison and Richard Steele. In the hands of

Addison and Steele, a sub-genre called the 'periodical essay' became very popular.

The essay has been flourishing since then thanks to writers such as Charles Lamb, William Hazlitt, Thomas de Quincey, Samuel Taylor Coleridge, Lord Macaulay, Leigh Hunt, Thomas Carlyle, John Ruskin, Matthew Arnold, Walter Pater, R.L. Stevenson, G.K. Chesterton, Hilaire Belloc, E.V. Lucas, Robert Lynd, and several others.

Features of the essay

- The modern essay tends to limit its length and range as far as the treatment of the subject goes. When the essay grows too long and attempts an exhaustive view of the subject, it ceases to be an essay and the term 'dissertation' or 'thesis' could be applied to it. The difference between the essay and the dissertation is that the essay is addressed to the lay person while the latter is for the consumption of the specialist.
- An essay does not attempt to give the reader an exhaustive or comprehensive understanding of its subject. According to the British author William Henry Hudson, 'selection and the proper distribution of emphasis will ... be found among the elementary principles of essay writing'. A good essay does not attempt too much.
- In spite of being only about a part of a subject, a good essay nevertheless gives the reader a sense of completeness in its treatment.
- The subject matter of the essay is unlimited and the form could cover a vast range of topics.

Let us now take a look at some well-known types of literary essays.

Aphoristic essay

It was Francis Bacon who was responsible for making the essay popular in England. In his hands, the subjective and self-revealing essays of Montaigne (which were his inspiration) underwent a sea change. Bacon's essays were highly objective and impersonal. In them, Bacon does not reveal himself, but offers counsel in short, crisp sentences that sound like aphorisms (sayings or maxims). Some examples of his aphorisms are: 'Imagination was given to compensate him for what he is not; a sense of humour to console him for what he is'; 'Reading maketh a full man; and writing an exact man'.

His essays contain a series of sentences like the ones quoted above. They fall like the strokes of a hammer without any literary frills and flounces. As a result, Bacon has been criticised as being abrupt and rugged. Some of his best essays are 'Of Truth', 'Of Friendship' and 'Of Revenge'.

Personal essay

The style is informal in such essays, and the author shares his views with the reader in an intimate manner. The subjects of such essays are usually everyday happenings rather than heavy matters like politics or spirituality. One could compare the personal essay to the lyric, which is another expression of personal feelings and emotions. The personal essay is autobiographical in nature, reflecting the author's inner thoughts and feelings.

Montaigne was the father of the personal essay. He wrote two volumes of essays that talk about his experiences in life and reflect his views on topics such as 'idleness' and 'lying'. In the hands of Charles Lamb, the personal essay scaled new heights. He wrote about the people he knew and about events from his own life. He had an excellent style of writing, taking his readers through a roller coaster ride of emotions. He combined humour, sentiment and common sense in an inimitable style. Some of the best examples of the personal essay can be found in the two collections by Lamb—*Essays of Elia* and *The Last Essays of Elia*. Other writers who wrote in a similar style include Leigh Hunt, Thomas De Quincey and William Hazlitt.

CHARACTER SKETCH

The character sketch is a brief but detailed description of the appearance and habits of either an individual or a generalised type. The intention is to amuse readers and to praise or satirise the person or type being described. This kind of writing became very popular in the earlier part of the seventeenth century. Examples of the 'character' (as such essays was called) include Thomas Overbury's 'A Good Wife' and 'A Drunken Dutchman Resident in England', and Joseph Hall's 'The Witless Gallant' and 'Of the Flatterer'. The vogue for such descriptions even extended to places and institutions; for example, John Milton's 'Character of the Long Parliament'.

The classical Greek writer Theophrastus (371–287BCE) pioneered this form. During the Renaissance, classical writers were rediscovered and imitated. The development of drama (which depicted various types of characters) was influenced by character writing. This close connection between character writers and dramatists is obvious when we study the plays of Ben Jonson, whose plays depict the vices and virtues of men and women. In the seventeenth century, character sketches, with their detailed descriptions of various types of personalities, suited the growing taste for satire. In the eighteenth century, many essays by Addison and Steele may be seen as extended character sketches, and count as among the last popular examples of this form.

Critical Essay

A critical essay is an essay that evaluates, discusses and interprets literary works. It was John Dryden who made this type of essay popular. His critical writing began as early as 1664, when he wrote a preface to his first play, *The Rival Ladies.* Many of Dryden's prefaces, as well as his *Essay on Dramatic Poesy* (which is in the form of a dialogue), are excellent examples of the critical essay. He could be considered the first literary critic in the English language. (Philip Sidney's *Apology* was not strictly literary criticism, as it focused more on defending poets and poetry.) In the seventeenth century, literary works were discussed and reviewed in coffee houses. During the Neoclassical period, several critical essays were written. Samuel Johnson was another eminent man of letters who wrote critical essays.

Periodical Essay

A periodical essay is an essay that appears in a journal or a periodical. This form rose to prominence in the early eighteenth century, which witnessed the growth of journalism. It was very well suited for social and literary criticism and for character studies.

Daniel Defoe's *Review* was the earliest periodical featuring essays, although the periodical essay form was made popular by the journals *The Tatler* and *The Spectator*, managed by Richard Steele and Joseph Addison. These journals contained essays that held up a mirror to the vanities, vices and foibles of contemporary society. The essays were intended 'to enliven morality with wit, and to temper wit with morality' (Addison). George Saintsbury, in his *Short History of English Literature,* pointed out that 'they taught the eighteenth century how it should, and especially how it should not, behave in public places, from churches to theatres; what books it should like, and how it should like them; how it should treat its lovers, mistresses, husbands, wives, parents, and friends'. Other famous essayists who employed this form include Dr Johnson (who contributed regularly to *The Rambler* and *The Idler*) and Oliver Goldsmith (whose series 'Citizen of the World' appeared in *The Public Ledger*).

4

Prose: Fiction

The Elements of Fiction

The novel and the short story are made of the same elements as drama—plot, characters, dialogue, setting, and so on. The nineteenth-century American writer Francis Marion Crawford called the novel 'pocket theatre'. However, unlike drama, the novel and the short story are pure literary forms that are not dependent upon the conditions of the stage and the performance of the actors.

PLOT

Loose plot and organic plot

Plot could be defined as a series of events developed in a meaningful manner. Based on the structure of the plot, one may categorise it as either a 'loose plot' or an 'organic plot'. In a story with a loose plot, a series of separate incidents are strung together. Often, when setting out to write the story, the author herself/himself is not aware of the direction it might eventually take. Loose plots are often seen in picaresque novels (see page 114). The main reason a novel of loose plot is regarded a 'novel', and not a collection of short stories, is the protagonist, whose presence is the common factor in all the incidents that form the plot of the story. Examples of novels with loose plots are Daniel Defoe's *Robinson Crusoe* (1719), Charles Dickens's *The Pickwick Papers* (1836), and William Makepeace Thackeray's *Vanity Fair* (1848).

In a story with an organic plot, the incidents are connected to each other and there is a gradual development of the story by by the author. A good example of this would be the novels of P.G. Wodehouse. In order to write such a story, the author should have a clear idea of the plot at the beginning itself. Examples of novels with organic plots are Henry Fielding's *Tom Jones* (1749) and Charles Dickens's *Bleak House* (1853). One cannot, however, apply such distinctions too rigidly and compartmentalise novels accordingly. There could be a lot of overlapping in a novelist's treatment of her/his story. For instance, there could be a lot of episodic material in an organic novel. In the very novels given as examples above, there are many incidents that do not form a part of the organic design of the story.

One should not conclude that a story with an organic plot is superior to one with a loose plot. In fact, there are two significant drawbacks to a story with a highly organised plot. First, the various twists and turns of the story could be too mechanically put together, leaving the reader with a slight sense of dissatisfaction at the laborious perfectness with which the story is narrated. The second drawback is the artificial manner in which all the threads of the narrative are tied up in the end. A novelist might often resort to highly contrived means such as coincidence, the death of one of the characters in a love triangle, the discovery of wills, or the reuniting of long-separated twins/siblings. A good plot should unravel the story naturally and the narrative should be free from artifice as much as possible.

Simple plot and compound plot

Another important aspect of plot is the study of the unity in its structure. The plot of a novel may be simple or compound. In a simple plot, there is one story only, whereas a compound (or multiple) plot features several stories woven together. This is true of plot in drama too. An example of a novel with a simple plot could be Chetan Baghat's *Two States* (2009).

Other examples of stories with simple plots would include fairy tales (such as 'Red Riding Hood') or detective fiction (such as Conan Doyle's Sherlock Holmes stories or Agatha Christie's Hercule Poirot stories). Novels such as Thackeray's *Vanity Fair,* George Eliot's *Middlemarch* (1874) and Leo Tolstoy's *Anna Karenina* (1877) have multiple plots that are not fused together. The different strands seem to exist independently with little effect upon one another. An excellent example of a novel of compound plot is Rohinton Mistry's *A Fine Balance* (1995), in which the individual stories of four diverse characters are fused together to form a most absorbing story.

NARRATIVE TECHNIQUE

The method of narration is another significant element of fiction. The word 'narrative' is derived from a Latin word meaning 'to tell'. How a story is told is an important way of studying fiction. To create a good narrative, the author needs to select the incidents carefully and create some connection between a series of events. A narrative is made up of dramatised incidents, descriptions of people and places, dialogue, reporting of past events, philosophical ruminations of the author or of one of the characters, and commentaries on society. It is the narrator who weaves all these things together. When we read a story, our attention is focused by the narrator's manner of presenting the story. This is known as **point of view**. The analysis and identification of point of view is the key to the discussion of the different methods of narration. There are three modes of narration—the first-person, the second-person, and the third-person.

First-person narrative

In a narrative told from a first-person perspective, the author tells the story through a character who refers to herself or himself as 'I'. This person is generally a character in the story.

See, for example, the following extract from Herman Melville's *Moby-Dick* (1851):

> Call me Ishmael. Some years ago—never mind how long precisely—having little or no money in my purse, and nothing particular to interest me on shore, I thought I would sail about a little and see the watery part of the world.

When a character in the story is the narrator, we can know only what this person observes and hears about the other characters. The entire story is unfolded to us from what this one character chooses to tell us. An example of this type of narrative is Emily Brontë's *Wuthering Heights* (1847), where the entire story is narrated as seen from the point of view of the housekeeper, Nellie Dean. She is able to narrate only those incidents that occurred while she was present, or which she knows about through others. Thus we do not know anything about how Hindley Earnshaw met his wife or about his wedding, since Nellie knows nothing about it. We learn about Isabella Linton's troubled marriage with Heathcliff only through the letter she writes to Nellie.

Second-person narrative

In the second-person narrative, the narrator addresses the protagonist or another important character by the second-person pronoun, 'you'. See, for example, the opening lines of Jay McInerney's *Bright Lights, Big City* (1984), the most famous example of this mode in English literature:

> You are not the kind of guy who would be at a place like this at this time of the morning. But here you are, and you cannot say the terrain is entirely unfamiliar, although the details are fuzzy.

The second-person point of view is extremely rare when compared to the first-person and the third-person modes. (This mode is more common to song lyrics or to nonfiction manuals such as self-help books, cookbooks or guidebooks.) The French novel *Second Thoughts* (1957) by Michel Butor is another example of a novel written from the second-person point of view. Other novelists have attempted the mode in limited sections of their novels, for example, Italo Calvino in his Italian postmodern narrative *If on a Winter's Night a Traveller* (1979) and the Scottish writer Iain Banks in *A Song of Stone* (1997).

Third-person narrative

In a third-person narrative, the narrator refers to the characters as 'he', 'she', 'they', or by name. In other words, the narrator is not a character. Take a look at this extract from George Orwell's *Nineteen Eighty-Four* (1949) which aptly demonstrates the mode:

> It was a bright cold day in April, and the clocks were striking thirteen. Winston Smith, his chin nuzzled into his breast in an effort to escape the vile wind, slipped quickly through the glass doors of Victory Mansions, though not quickly enough to prevent a swirl of gritty dust from entering along with him.

The novels of Jane Austen are good examples of third-person narratives. The third-person narrative mode could be studied under two headings: omniscient and limited.

An author who adopts the role of a **third-person omniscient** narrator assumes a vantage point, and is not only able to recount the action thoroughly and reliably but is also able to enter the mind of any character in the work in order to reveal his or her thoughts, feelings, and beliefs directly to the reader.

The novels of Leo Tolstoy, such as *War and Peace* (1869), are good examples of this.

An author using the **third-person limited** point of view recounts the story through the eyes of a single character or a few of his characters and presents the story as seen from their point of view. In this mode of storytelling, we usually learn a great deal about the private history and the thoughts of one character in the story. Henry James called such a character the 'focus' or the 'centre of consciousness'. In James's novel *What Maisie Knew* (1897), the story is recounted solely from the point of view of a child. The limited point of view gradually developed into the sophisticated stream of consciousness technique (see page 127) in the twentieth century.

CHARACTERISATION

A character is a person or animal who takes part in the action of a literary work. Creating life-like characters is vital to the craft of fiction. Characters that are realistically delineated remain in our memory long after the book is read. One can never forget characters like Sydney Carton in *A Tale of Two Cities*, or Darcy and Mrs Bennet in Austen's *Pride and Prejudice*, or Scarlett O'Hara and Rhett Butler in Margaret Mitchell's *Gone with the Wind*.

Types of characters

In terms of the importance of their roles, a character who plays an important role in a story is called a **major character**, while a character who does not play a significant role is called a **minor character**. For example, in Mark Twain's *The Adventures of Tom Sawyer* (1876), Tom Sawyer and the antagonist (see below) Injun Joe are major characters, while Widow Douglas and Judge Thatcher are minor characters.

In terms of their roles, a character who plays the central role in a story is called the **protagonist** and the one who opposes her/him is called the **antagonist**. Dorothy is the protagonist of L. Frank Baum's children's novel *The Wonderful Wizard of Oz* (1900), while the Wicked Witch of the West is the main antagonist. A story may have more than just one protagonist or antagonist; for example, J.R.R. Tolkien's *The Lord of the Rings* (1954).

In terms of their complexity, the English novelist E.M. Forster distinguished between flat and round characters. A character who remains uncomplicated and unchanging from the beginning to the end of a work is known as a **flat character** or a **static character**. These characters are predictable and there is no development or growth in their behaviour. Examples of such characters are Mrs Bennet from Austen's *Pride and Prejudice* (1813) and Mrs Micawber from Dickens's *David Copperfield* (1850). A character who changes and develops in the course of the novel is known as a **round character** or a **dynamic character**. Examples of round characters are Mr Darcy (*Pride and Prejudice*) and David Copperfield (*David Copperfield*).

Direct and indirect method of characterisation

The presentation and delineation of characters may be done either directly or indirectly. In the **direct** method, the writer *tells* us directly what a character is like or what a person's motives are. For example, in her novel *The Mill on the Floss* (1860), George Eliot tells us directly what kind of person Mrs Tulliver is:

> Mrs Tulliver was what is called a good-tempered person,—never cried, when she was a baby, on any slighter ground than hunger and pins; and from the cradle upward had been healthy, fair, plump, and dull-witted; in short, the flower of her family for beauty and amiability.

This method is not favoured by modern writers, who prefer the **indirect** method where readers discover for themselves the nature of the characters (the writer *shows*, as opposed to telling us). The writer stands apart and allows his characters to reveal themselves through speech, appearance, thoughts, or actions. The readers interpret for themselves the kind of person they are meeting in the novel. In the indirect method, characterisation is mainly done through dialogue and action. What a character says and the manner of saying it reveal her/his nature. Another way of interpreting a character through dialogue is from what other characters say about the given character. Apart from dialogue, a character reveals herself/himself through her/his actions too. Examples of indirect characterisation abound in modern novels and short stories, such as those by James Joyce, John Steinbeck and Katherine Mansfield.

SETTING

The next important element in fiction is setting, that is, the time and place of action. Setting is the combination of place, historical time, and social milieu. It provides the context and the general background for the characters and the plot. Setting greatly adds to the attractiveness and literary value of a work of fiction. The general setting of a work may differ from the specific setting of an individual scene or event.

The author provides a geographical location in which the story takes place. The action of the plot could happen in a bygone age or in the distant future. It is through the setting that the reader learns about the men, manners and climate of the place being described. A novel may faithfully reflect the peculiar customs of a particular class or society, if relevant to the story. A setting can create expectations in the reader, be a source of conflict for the characters, and add layers to the themes of a work. Some authors do thorough research before describing the setting of a work.

The setting of a literary work could be real, as in James Joyce's *Ulysses* (1922), which is set in contemporary Dublin, or imaginary, as in the countries of Lilliput and Brobdingnag in Jonathan Swift's *Gulliver's Travels* (1726). A story may be set in the past, present, future, or in an alternate history. *Midnight's Children* (1981) by Salman Rushdie is set in the Indian subcontinent immediately before and after the independence and partition of India, while *The Hunger Games* (2008) by Suzanne Collins is set in a dystopian North America many years into the future.

Functions of setting

Setting as background

Setting provides a background and tells us where and when the story takes place. A good setting helps to make the story real and believable. John Fowles opens his novel *The French Lieutenant's Woman* (1969) with the following words:

> An easterly is the most disagreeable wind in Lyme Bay—Lyme Bay being that largest bite from the underside of England's outstretched southwestern leg—and a person of curiosity could at once have deduced several strong probabilities about the pair who began to walk down the quay at Lyme Regis, the small but ancient eponym of the inbite, one incisively sharp and blustery morning in the late March of 1867.

This opening line immediately tells us that the story is set in the mid-nineteenth century in an old port town on the southwestern coast of Victorian England.

Setting and character

The setting can be used to tell us something about the people who belong to it, and can even act as symbols for characters. In Emily Brontë's *Wuthering Heights* (1847), we are given a detailed description of the drawing room in Thrushcross Grange, the Linton residence:

> … it was a beautiful—a splendid place carpeted with crimson, and crimson-covered chairs and tables, and a pure white ceiling bordered by gold, shower of glass-drops hanging in silver chains from the centre, and shimmering with little soft tapers.

The affluent setting of the Linton household reflects the nature, moods and attitude of the Lintons—cultured, a little spoilt, calm and moral. Contrast this with the residence of the Earnshaws and of Heathcliff, which is located on a barren moor:

> Wuthering Heights is the name of Mr Heathcliff's dwelling ... descriptive of the atmospheric tumult to which [it] is exposed in stormy weather … One may guess the power of the north wind blowing over the edge by the excessive slant of a few stunted firs at the end of the house, and by a range of gaunt thorns all stretching their limbs one way, as if craving alms of the sun ... the architect [built] it strong. The narrow windows are deeply set in the wall, and the corners defended with large jutting stones ... grotesque carving lavished over the front ...

The wild, strong, harsh and uninviting setting reflects the passionate, amoral, cruel, selfish and malevolent nature of Heathcliff. The two settings symbolise the conflict between the main characters. Fittingly, Catherine Earnshaw, who moves from one setting to the other, is at the centre of this conflict.

Setting and atmosphere

Setting can also be used to affect our feelings. Some settings can make us feel uneasy or afraid. When an author describes a haunted house on a lonely night, descriptions such as that of a branch scraping a window or a dog howling can make a chill creep up the spine of the reader. The setting can also be used to create a happy mood, through descriptions of bright sunshine and birds chirping on the trees. In the short story 'The Fall of the House of Usher' (1839), Edgar Allan Poe brilliantly uses the setting to create an atmosphere of vague uneasiness and the dread of imminent doom.

Setting and conflict

In some stories, the setting even performs the function of providing the conflict. For instance, there are stories in which the protagonist fights against a physical attribute of the world around her/him, such as a drought, the heat of a desert, or a calamity like a shipwreck or an earthquake. In *Journey to the Centre of the Earth* (1864) by Jules Verne, the narrative focuses on the adventures of a group of people trying to survive the natural hazards of the novel's setting.

Setting and emotion

An interesting use of setting is to indicate the mood of the characters: when they are sad, the weather is gloomy; when they experience inner turmoil, there is a storm; when they are happy, it is bright and sunny. Writers use rhetorical devices like **pathetic fallacy** (attributing human feelings to inanimate objects) to achieve this. Depicting nature as sympathising with man or reflecting the emotions of characters is a common dramatic device, and can be seen, for example, in the novels of Charles Dickens. Sometimes, instead of symbolically paralleling human emotion, the author may create an effect of contrast by showing nature as being uncaring or indifferent to the sufferings of man, as in Thomas Hardy's *The Return of the Native* (1878).

DIALOGUE

The well-managed use of dialogue is vital to the success of a novel or a short story, for it serves many functions. The author can use dialogue instead of narration to relate the action. It can advance the story by moving the plot forward. A story gains dramatic interest when the narrative is interspersed with dialogue. In the hands of a skilful author, well-written dialogue can be used to provide exposition, create conflict, change the pace of the narrative, establish mood, indicate the passage of time, and illuminate themes.

Good dialogue helps to bring characters to life. Characters reveal themselves through speech. Hence, dialogue is used extensively by an author in the delineation of character. It is not only the words uttered by a particular character, but also what other characters say about her/him, that helps us in understanding that character. A writer could simply tell us about a character's emotions and motivations; but when these are revealed through the character's speech, it connects the reader directly with that character. Thus, dialogue helps to establish a deeper bond between reader and character. The idiosyncratic speech rhythms peculiar to certain individuals, if captured accurately by the author, can make them come alive. We are able to immediately identify characters like Miss Bates in Austen's *Emma* (1815), Jim in Mark Twain's *Huckleberry Finn* (1884), and Waterfall Venkamma in Raja Rao's *Kanthapura* (1938). Charles Dickens was particularly good at revealing a character's socioeconomic background simply through the character's manner of speaking.

Short Story

A short story could be defined as a short piece of fiction that concentrates on a single incident, a single character (or very few characters), or the creation of a single effect or impression.

It is marked by an economy of expression and tightness of form, and can be read in one sitting. The defining factor of the short story is that it should be short. With the growth of various periodicals, the short story has become the most widely read literary form.

Origin and growth

Short prose fiction is one of the oldest forms of literature. The earliest examples of the short story can be seen in the stories written in 3000BCE in ancient Egypt. The parables of the Bible are other early examples of short prose fiction. These impart moral lessons to the reader. Yet another example of this genre is the Sanskrit collection *Panchatantra* from India (circa third century BCE). Other examples from the East include the Arabic collections *Thousand and One Nights* (from the eighth century CE onwards) and *The Book of Sindbad* (circa tenth century CE). Two of the most well-known collections of early short stories from the West are the *Decameron*, a collection of a hundred tales by the Italian writer Giovanni Boccaccio, and *The Canterbury Tales,* a book containing twenty-four stories by the English poet Geoffrey Chaucer. Both were written in the fourteenth century.

There were several early forms of the short story such as the **fable** (a short story conveying a moral, in which the characters are animals with human qualities; for example, the Greek fables of Aesop and the Sanskrit collection *Hitopadesha*), the **fabliau** (a short, satirical or comic tale in verse, known for its bawdiness; for example, the medieval French tales 'Gombert and the Two Clerks' and 'The Snow Baby'), and the **folktale** (short stories of unknown origin which exist mostly in the oral form; for example, English folklore related to Robin Hood, and Indian tales of the cleverness of Birbal or the wit of Tenali Raman). An **exemplum** is an anecdote with a moral. In the Middle Ages, there were many books of exempla, which priests used in their sermons. A literary example of an exemplum is Chaucer's 'The Pardoner's Tale' (from *The Canterbury Tales*) which illustrates the moral that 'love of wealth is the root of all evil'.

The short story was recognised as a major literary form in the nineteenth century. The form first became popular not in England, but in America. Even there, the term 'short story' was used only in the 1880s. Edgar Allan Poe was the first important author to analyse this form and discuss the various effects that a short story could have, such as surprise and fear. Other American writers include Nathaniel Hawthorne, Herman Melville and O. Henry. Some examples of well-known short stories are 'The Legend of Sleepy Hollow' by Washington Irving, 'The Gift of the Magi' by O. Henry, 'The Necklace' by Guy de Maupassant, and 'The Secret Life of Walter Mitty' by James Thurber. Famous collections of short stories include Poe's *Tales of Mystery and Imagination* (published posthumously in 1902), *Dubliners* (1914) by James Joyce, and *Interpreter of Maladies* (1999) by Jhumpa Lahiri .

Today, the short story is a very popular form all over the world and appears in almost every language. Famous writers of short stories include Anton Chekhov, Arthur Conan Doyle, D.H. Lawrence, Leo Tolstoy, Ernest Hemingway, Flannery O'Connor, Franz Kafka, R.K. Narayan, Ray Bradbury, Saadat Hasan Manto, Isaac Asimov, Khushwant Singh, and Alice Munroe, to name just a few.

Features of the short story

- The short story is a distinct literary form. It must not be regarded as a shortened novel.
- The short story contains all the major elements of fiction, such as plot, characters, dialogue and setting.
- The short story tends to focus on a single plot. It concentrates on one character or a very small set of

characters, in a single setting (or, at the most, two or three), and the main action covers a short period of time.
- While the plot is usually not as complicated as that of a novel, the short story form can handle as wide a range of simple to heavy themes as the novel.
- The short story is a concentrated form of prose narrative. The writing is economical and dense. There are no leisurely descriptions as found in the novel (unless it serves a specific purpose). Writers whittle down anything that does not contribute to the overall effect that they intend to produce in the reader.
- The denouement (the final unfolding of the plot, see page 43) is swift, and the ending is usually abrupt and open to interpretation. The short story can end in suspense, with a surprise, an anticlimax, an epiphany, or in many other ways.

Novel

A novel could be defined as a long work of prose fiction containing characters, incidents and a plot. The word 'novel' comes from the Italian 'novella' meaning a 'piece of news' or 'tale', and was first applied to tales like Boccaccio's *Decameron*, which were very popular in the fourteenth century. Though it originated much after other genres like poetry and drama, it is one of the most popular forms of literature today.

Origin and growth

The roots of the novel form may be traced to ancient Greece and Rome. The Greeks wrote stories called 'romances' that described tales of adventure and love. Roman examples of this form include the Latin works *Satyricon* (first century CE) by Gaius Petronius and *Metamorphoses* (also known as *The Golden Ass*, first century CE) by Lucius Apuleius. Other forerunners of the form are Thomas Malory's Middle English prose romance, *Morte d'Arthur* (published posthumously in 1485); Philip Sidney's pastoral romance, *Arcadia* (written in the late sixteenth century); Thomas Nashe's picaresque narrative, *The Unfortunate Traveller* (1594); and Miguel de Cervantes's Spanish masterpiece, *Don Quixote* (early seventeenth century).

Critics are divided in their opinion as to which work could be credited as being the first novel in English. Many consider Daniel Defoe's *Robinson Crusoe* (1719) as the first English novel. Others dismiss the claim as they feel it is not a proper novel, but just a series of episodes, as is Defoe's next work, *Moll Flanders* (1722). Some critics believe the distinction should go to Samuel Richardson's *Pamela* (1740), as it contains a well-developed plot. The popularity of *Pamela* paved the way for other novelists. Henry Fielding, Tobias Smollett and Laurence Sterne number among the great novelists of the eighteenth century.

The popularity of the novel grew with the passing of every century. In the nineteenth century, many great novels were written by authors such as Walter Scott, Jane Austen, the Brontë sisters, George Eliot, William Makepeace Thackeray, Charles Dickens, Anthony Trollope, Thomas Hardy, and Henry James, to name just a few. In the twentieth century, the novel saw tremendous changes and became a highly sophisticated art form in the hands of writers such as Joseph Conrad, Virginia Woolf, James Joyce, John Fowles, Graham Greene, and William Golding. In the twenty-first century, novels are being written in almost every corner of the globe, and novelists continue to experiment with various styles, plots and techniques.

Features of the novel

There are many different kinds and genres of novels. However, four main features distinguish the novel as a unique literary form.

- The novel is a narrative. It essentially tells a story that is narrated by one of the characters or by an omniscient narrator (the author). In this it differs from the drama, in which the story is unfolded through dialogue on the stage.
- The novel is written in prose rather than in verse (though there are very rare exceptions, such as Vikram Seth's *The Golden Gate*, which is written entirely in verse). The fact that a novel is almost always in prose distinguishes it as a form from long narrative poems.
- The novel is a work of fiction, which differentiates it from other forms of prose such as biographies, autobiographies and histories.
- The novel is an extended prose narrative, unlike the short story which is much smaller in scope and length. The novel typically runs into several hundred pages and covers a larger period of time, with more action and characters than a short story.

Picaresque novel

The word 'picaresque' is derived from the Spanish word 'pícaro' meaning 'rogue' or 'rascal'. This type of novel originated in the sixteenth century and became very popular in the seventeenth and eighteenth centuries.

Features of a picaresque novel

- In a picaresque novel, a travelling hero usually finds herself/himself in different kinds of situations, meets a variety of characters, and has several extraordinary experiences.
- There is little or no plot, and the novel has a simple, loose, episodic structure.
- The protagonist is clever, likeable and usually someone from the middle or lower class. The author takes the hero through several ups and downs in life.

- Though characters are prominently drawn, there is little character development. The story (action) is given more importance.
- The novel is narrated in a satirical and humorous manner, often in the first-person mode.

In Tobias Smollett's *The Adventures of Roderick Random* (1748), the hero, Roderick, meets a variety of odd people on his long journey to London, and has a series of misadventures along the way. He later joins the navy and has further escapades. Roderick has far too many adventures than is possible for any person to have in one life, but the author does not bother about the credibility of such incidents. Smollett is only interested in giving his readers a broad picture of the life of his times. Other examples of picaresque narratives include Henry Fielding's *Tom Jones* (1749), Voltaire's *Candide* (1759), and Saul Bellow's *The Adventures of Augie March* (1953).

Epistolary novel

This was one of the earliest types of novel and was very popular in the eighteenth century. In this type of fiction, the story is told entirely through letters sent by the characters involved in the action or by those who are observing it.

Features of an epistolary novel

- The plot unfolds as the characters write letters to each other (or to the reader) to narrate the events that have taken place.
- Multiple points of view can be revealed directly to the reader without any third-person authorial intervention.
- The letters, apart from being the means of narrating the story, also help in reflecting the psychological and moral conflicts of their writers.

- Since the letters provide an intimate look into a character's thoughts and feelings, the epistolary novel is often seen as the forerunner of the psychological novel (see page 126).
- This form of the novel also depends on other documents like diary entries, telegrams and newspaper clippings to develop the plot. An excellent example of this is Bram Stoker's *Dracula* (1897).
- The drawback of this type of novel is that it suffers from a certain amount of artificiality. In addition to this, some sense of immediacy is lost when describing action.

Samuel Richardson's *Pamela* (1740) and *Clarissa* (1748) are good examples of the epistolary novel. The epistolary novel has been revived throughout English literary history by writers who recognised its potential. Prominent examples include Jean Webster's *Daddy-Long-Legs* (1912), C.S. Lewis's *The Screwtape Letters* (1942), Saul Bellow's *Herzog* (1964), Alice Walker's *The Color Purple* (1982), and Aravind Adiga's *The White Tiger* (2008). The epistolary form has also been parodied, most notably in Henry Fielding's *Shamela* (1741), which mocks Richardson's *Pamela*.

Historical novel

In this form of fiction, the author attempts to reconstruct history imaginatively, and sometimes romantically.

Features of a historical novel

- This novel is set in a past historical period, and describes the events and manners of that period. Through the imaginative recreation of a bygone age, historical novels add colour to the events of the past and bring them to life.
- It may be peopled by both real and imaginary characters. Historical personalities may play either a major or a minor part in the action.

- Authors of historical novels extensively research the period they intend to depict. They pay attention to minute details regarding dress, manner of speaking, food habits, customs, and other social aspects that were prevalent during that age.
- Close attention is paid to the historical events of that time, which are usually incorporated into the plot.
- Writers try to avoid **anachronisms** (the inclusion of some action or object in a work which could not have existed or occurred in the historical period being depicted; a famous example is Shakespeare's reference to a clock in his play *Julius Caesar*). Sir Walter Scott (who made the historical novel popular), although an excellent storyteller, is guilty of several anachronisms in his novels.

Walter Scott's *Waverley* (1814), *Rob Roy* (1817), and *Ivanhoe* (1820) are some of the most memorable novels in this genre. The popularity of the historical novel, even in the present day, may be seen in the several examples we have of this form—*The Three Musketeers* (1844) by Alexandre Dumas, *A Tale of Two Cities* (1859) by Charles Dickens, *War and Peace* (1869) by Leo Tolstoy, *I, Claudius* (1934) by Robert Graves, *Flashman* (1969) by George MacDonald Fraser, *The Other Boleyn Girl* (2001) by Philippa Gregory, and the 'Empire of the Moghul' series (2009–13) by Alex Rutherford, to name a few.

SENTIMENTAL NOVEL

In the eighteenth century, the word 'sentimental' meant having refined or elevated feelings. It is this meaning that we must keep in mind while studying this genre. The sentimental novel is also known as the **novel of sensibility**.

Features of a sentimental novel

- As a literary genre, it celebrates the intellectual and emotional aspects of **sentimentalism** (giving importance to feelings over reason) and **sensibility** (being acutely aware of and responsive towards stimuli and emotions). These were fashionable attitudes in eighteenth-century poetry and fiction, and may be seen as a reaction to the rationalism of the Augustan Age.

- The novel relies on an emotional response from both the characters and the readers by depicting scenes of suffering and tenderness.
- The focus is more on furthering emotional feelings rather than the action. As a result, the readers are presented with characters who serve as models of patience and endurance.
- The novels often shone a spotlight on the weaker sections of society, such as orphans and the poor, or on the terrible conditions of the prison system of the time.
- The sentimental novel played an important role in creating awareness towards the downtrodden section of society and helped pave the way for the humanitarian movements of the eighteenth century.

Samuel Richardson's *Pamela* (1740) depicts the importance of a love that transcends the physical. Other important examples of sentimental novels include Oliver Goldsmith's *Vicar of Wakefield* (1766), Laurence Sterne's *A Sentimental Journey Through France and Italy* (1768), Henry Mackenzie's *The Man of Feeling* (1771), and Johann Wolfgang von Goethe's German novel *The Sorrows of Young Werther* (1774).

Domestic novel

The domestic novel or the **conduct novel** is a subgenre of the sentimental novel that became popular in the early nineteenth century. This novel made use of sentimentalism to convey its message to the readers.

Features of a domestic novel

- The plot centres on a female protagonist who is the embodiment of either the sacrificing angel or the simple practical woman. This woman is contrasted with a passive or an ignorant woman.
- The heroine goes through several trials and tribulations, suffering abuse from powerful people, before she discovers herself and gains some measure of independence or self-sufficiency.
- The heroine has to strike a balance between society's expectations of sacrifice from a woman and the fulfilment of her own desires, while trying her best not to succumb to the pressures all around her.
- The novel usually ends with a wedding. The heroine either reforms the rakish male or marries a dependable man who is equal to her.
- The language is usually sentimental in order to evoke the sympathy of the readers.

Examples of domestic novels include *A New-England Tale* (1822) by Catharine Sedgwick, *The Lamplighter* (1854) by Maria Cummins, and *The Old Homestead* (1855) by Ann Stephens.

GOTHIC NOVEL

The term 'Gothic' originally referred to the Goths, an early medieval Germanic tribe, and later came to signify 'Germanic' and 'medieval'. The Gothic novel is a type of **romance** (a prose narrative dealing with events remote from everyday life) that was popular in the late eighteenth and early nineteenth centuries. It is a very distinct form with interesting features and has been a great influence upon fiction.

Features of a gothic novel

- Gothic novels narrate tales of mystery and horror aimed at startling the readers.
- The setting usually includes haunted castles with secret passages, winding staircases, dungeons, and caves. American writers of Gothic fiction often set the story in a distant place and in a bygone age, such as medieval Europe.
- The atmosphere is threatening or gloomy. The novelists created a mood of suspense and evoked the fear of the unknown.
- It includes supernatural elements (such as ghosts) and strange, eerie happenings. Other common features are disturbing visions, frightening dreams and foreboding omens.
- The heroine is beautiful and virtuous. She is often oppressed by a powerful male figure.
- The mode of narration is sentimental or melodramatic, and the characters often display strong emotions.
- The feelings of pity and terror aroused by this novel do not have a cathartic effect, but are to be enjoyed for their own sake.

This type of fiction was made popular by Horace Walpole's *Castle of Otranto* (1764). Ann Radcliffe's *Mysteries of Udolpho* (1794) and Matthew Gregory Lewis's *The Monk* (1796) were important formative influences on the genre. Mary Shelley's *Frankenstein* (1818) is a popular example of the form. Edgar Allan Poe developed this style in the United States. Other famous Gothic novels include Robert Louis Stevenson's *Strange Case of Dr Jekyll and Mr Hyde* (1886), Oscar Wilde's *The Picture of Dorian Gray* (1891), Bram Stoker's *Dracula* (1897), and Gaston Leroux's *The Phantom of the Opera* (1909–10).

Science Fiction Novel

Science fiction is a genre in which elements of science and technology play an integral part in the story. It is often shortened to 'SF'. Science fiction novels blend fantasy with science to create the sense of an alternate reality which seems quite possible.

Features of a science fiction novel

- By basing the plot and other story elements on actual scientific facts, principles and technology, science fiction creates an illusion of reality. However, the stories also often involve plausible laws or theories that are partly fictitious or speculative.
- The stories are usually set in the future, in space, on a different planet, in a different universe, in an alternate dimension, or in an alternate history.
- The novels depict situations that are different from the present or from the known past or the conceivable future.
- Science fiction narratives may involve elements such as dystopia, advanced technology, time travel, space travel, and extraterrestrial life.
- Science fiction novels often depict the effect of new scientific discoveries and advances in technology upon human beings.
- Novelists often use science fiction to comment on social and cultural issues such as class inequality, greed, war, political authoritarianism, the misuse of technology, the dangers of environmental exploitation, the ill effects of acquiring knowledge irrespective of consequences, and so on.

Mary Shelley's *Frankenstein* (1818) is one of the earliest novels to belong to this genre. The French writer Jules Verne and the English author H.G. Wells made this form very popular.

Verne authored *Journey to the Centre of the Earth* (1864), *From the Earth to the Moon* (1865) and *Twenty Thousand Leagues under the Sea* (1869), while Wells's famous novels are *The Time Machine* (1895), *The Invisible Man* (1897), and *The War of the Worlds* (1898). These are regarded as the classic works of science fiction. Other prominent writers of science fiction are Isaac Asimov (*Foundation*, 1951), Ray Bradbury (*Fahrenheit 451*, 1953), Robert A. Heinlein (*Stranger in a Strange Land*, 1961), Philip K. Dick (*Do Androids Dream of Electric Sheep?*, 1968) and Arthur C. Clarke (*Rendezvous with Rama*, 1973).

New Wave science fiction

This term, applied to certain works of science fiction written in the 1960s and 1970s, was borrowed from the French film movement known as the 'nouvelle vague'. The New Wave was a reaction to traditional science fiction, which was regarded as pulp fiction. The writers of the New Wave deliberately broke away from the traditions of popular science fiction. Importance was given to a high degree of stylistic experimentation and artistic merit, while scientific accuracy took a backseat. The writers' focus on literary experimentation with regard to both form and content was intended to 'elevate' science fiction as a serious literary form. Much of New Wave science fiction appeared in the English magazine *New Worlds*, edited by Michael Moorcock.

J.G. Ballard (*The Drowned World*, 1962), Philip José Farmer ('World of Tiers' series, 1965–93), and John Brunner (*Stand on Zanzibar*, 1968) are some of the prominent writers who belong to this genre. The New Wave also witnessed the emergence of several female writers such as Ursula K. Le Guin (*The Left Hand of Darkness*, 1969) and Joanna Russ (*The Female Man*, 1975).

Regional novel

A regional novel depicts a particular geographical area, and uses it and the people belonging to it as the basis for the plot.

Features of a regional novel

- The setting is an important feature in a regional novel. It is usually set in a rural or provincial area having a distinguishable life style.
- Such a novel emphasises and documents the culture, history, customs and speech of the region it is set in, with more focus than for mere background.

Maria Edgeworth's *Castle Rackrent* (1800) is believed to be the first regional novel in English. Famous regional novelists include Thomas Hardy, who recreated western England in many of his novels and revived the name 'Wessex'; the American novelist William Faulkner, who based his fictional region Yoknapatawpha County on the American South; the Indian writer R.K. Narayan, whose Malgudi was the setting of almost all his work; and the Canadian author Margaret Laurence, who set her stories in the fictional town of Manawaka.

Detective novel

Detective fiction has been a popular genre in the novel form ever since the nineteenth century. It is a distinct subgenre of **crime fiction**—stories that deal with crime, criminals, and their apprehension. (Other subgenres of crime fiction include the hardboiled novel, the police procedural, and the courtroom thriller.)

In detective fiction, the detective (along with the reader) is presented with an apparently insoluble crime and the case is slowly cracked. In the crime novel, on the other hand, the author shares with the reader the identity of the criminal at the very beginning, and the interest lies in following the detective's progress in identifying the culprit and in observing the culprit's attempts to escape from her/him.

Features of a detective novel

- An apparently perfect crime or murder is committed, which leaves the police baffled. The unsolvable nature of the crime keeps the reader interested. A sense of mystery is created, sometimes accompanied by tension or a sense of danger.
- The novel takes the reader through the process of the investigation of the crime by the protagonist, who eventually zeroes in on the culprit.
- The protagonist may be a professional or an amateur detective. Very often, the detective is an eccentric character with idiosyncratic mannerisms.
- The detective may have a confidant, who acts as a sounding board (and is usually a stand-in for the reader).
- The police and other authority figures are sometimes depicted as being either uncooperative or dim-witted.
- Multiple probable suspects, red herrings, and unsavoury characters are common features of such novels.
- The resolution is usually startling and unexpected. The detective explains how she/he logically arrived at the right solution.

Edgar Allan Poe, the American novelist, is considered to be the pioneer of this genre. His short story 'The Murders in the Rue Morgue' (1841) is considered to be the first modern detective story. Wilkie Collins's *The Moonstone* (1868) is usually considered to be the first English detective novel. The most famous detective to be created is, of course, Sherlock Holmes, who appeared for the first time in 1887 in the novel, *A Study in Scarlet* by Arthur Conan Doyle. G.K. Chesterton's Father Brown is another famous detective. Agatha Christie wrote several novels in this genre and created the detectives

Hercule Poirot and Miss Marple. *Murder on the Orient Express* (1934) is one of her most widely read books.

SOCIAL NOVEL

A social novel is one which focuses on a social, political or religious problem. It is also referred to as a **sociological novel**, **thesis novel**, **propaganda novel**, or **problem novel**.

Features of a social novel

- The social novel is didactic in purpose. The author's aim in such novels is to draw the attention of the public to the issue being discussed.
- The issues dealt with include social inequality (gender, race, or class prejudice), poverty, the problems of rapid industrialisation, child labour, violence against women, and so on.
- The protagonists of such novels are from the oppressed classes of society, and are shown in a sympathetic light.
- The novelist tries to move the reader by dramatising the effect of the above issues on the characters in the novel.

One of the earliest examples of such a novel is Charles Kingsley's *Alton Locke* (1850) in which he turned the spotlight on the nineteenth-century sweatshops where clothes were manufactured. Harriet Beecher Stowe's *Uncle Tom's Cabin* (1852) is another example. This novel was so successful in attracting the attention of the people to the savage practice of slavery, that it paved the way for the Civil War in America. Some other famous sociological novels are Charles Dickens's *Hard Times* (1854), Upton Sinclair's *The Jungle* (1906), Mulk Raj Anand's *Untouchable* (1935) and *Coolie* (1936), John Steinbeck's *The Grapes of Wrath* (1939), and Alan Paton's *Cry, the Beloved Country* (1948).

Proletarian novel

The **proletarian** is a member of the working class, the lowest economic class in society. The proletarian novel (also known as the **working class novel**) is a type of social novel which focuses on the problems of the working classes and is usually written by authors who are themselves from the working class. Its features are similar to that of the sociological novel. These novels usually have a strong anti-capitalist, political bent, and are often regarded as promoting political revolution.

Proletarian novels are often written by authors with socialist, communist or anarchist leanings. Proletarian fiction is prominent in Russian and Japanese literature. The best English example is Walter Greenwood's *Love on the Dole* (1933). Robert Cantwell's *Land of Plenty* (1934) is an American example.

Psychological Novel

The psychological novel is primarily concerned with the analysis of the spiritual, emotional and mental lives of the characters rather than with the plot. This type of novel came into vogue after the discoveries of Sigmund Freud and Carl Jung.

Features of a psychological novel

- The novelist's interest in human nature leads her/him into making an in-depth study of human relationships, thus giving a psychological slant to the story.
- The novel focuses on analysing the characters' motives which drive the action forward.
- Devices such as interior monologues and flashbacks are often used to explain the inner workings of the minds of the characters.

Henry James's novels display an ultrasensitive flair for analysing complex personalities. His work *The Portrait of a*

Lady (1881) is a psychological novel about a spirited American woman.

STREAM OF CONSCIOUSNESS NOVEL

Stream of consciousness is a narrative technique which attempts to capture all the emotions and thoughts which flow through a character's mind in a random manner. The term 'stream of consciousness' was coined by the American psychologist William James (brother of novelist Henry James) in his book *The Principles of Psychology* (1890). In literature, it is often used interchangeably with the term 'interior monologue'. Many modernist novels use this device to present before the reader the unfiltered thought processes of a character.

Features of a stream of consciousness novel

- The traditional concepts of plot and characterisation are given up.
- The standard techniques of description, narrative and dialogue are replaced with interior monologues.
- The author emphasises memory, intuition, sense perceptions and feelings, along with a character's thoughts.
- The focus is on capturing the fluidity of the inner life and depicting the myriad feelings and thoughts passing through a character's mind.
- These novels are often **anti-romantic** (a story featuring an unsure or indifferent protagonist who fails in her/his quest/journey).
- There is a great degree of artistic aloofness and impersonality on the part of the author.

Dorothy Richardson was among the first modernist writers to employ this technique. James Joyce's *Ulysses* (1922) and *Finnegans Wake* (1939), Virginia Woolf's *Mrs Dalloway*

(1925) and *To the Lighthouse* (1927), and William Faulkner's *The Sound and the Fury* (1929) are well-known examples of the stream of consciousness novel.

ANTINOVEL

The antinovel is an experimental form which breaks away from the traditional methods of storytelling. In it, the author makes no attempt to create the illusion of realism. The reader is not able to identify with the characters as in a traditional novel. The term was coined by the French philosopher Jean-Paul Sartre in 1948.

Features of an antinovel

- There is no well-defined plot. A number of diffused episodes are put together.
- There is little attempt at character development. The personality of a character may change abruptly.
- There is a great deal of detailed descriptions of objects.
- The author experiments with vocabulary, punctuation and syntax. There is a lot of repetition.
- There are variations in the sequence of time, and incidents may not be presented in chronological order.
- There are multiple endings and beginnings.
- Some extreme examples of this genre feature detachable pages, pages that can be shuffled like a pack of cards, blank pages, and coloured pages.

Laurence Sterne's *Tristram Shandy* (1759–67) may justifiably be regarded as a precursor to the antinovel. Notable examples of the antinovel form include are Jean-Paul Sartre's *Nausea* (1938), Albert Camus's *The Outsider* (1942), Philip Toynbee's *Tea with Mrs Goodman* (1947) and Alain Robbe-Grillet's *Jealousy* (1957).

NOUVEAU ROMAN

The *nouveau roman* (French for '**new novel**') was a French genre that emerged in the 1950s. There is very little difference between the antinovel and the new novel, and many works of *nouveau roman* could be classified as antinovels. The term '*nouveau roman*' became a part of critical jargon in the 1950s in France, after Alain Robbe-Grillet published his essays on the future of the novel form.

Nouveau roman novels concentrate on presenting precise, condensed physical descriptions of their subject, avoiding metaphors and similes. Plot, characterisation, and traditional narrative techniques and elements are rejected. Readers are challenged to interpret the story from the descriptions. These novels exhibit no fixed or consistent style: authors create a new style in each new novel. Prominent exponents of the form included Marguerite Duras, Alain Robbe-Grillet, Nathalie Sarraute, Claude Simon, Philippe Sollers, and Michel Butor. They had little in common besides an interest in avant-garde experimentation and the rejection of traditional modes of literary expression.

BILDUNGSROMAN

Bildungsroman is a genre in which the plot revolves around the psychological and moral growth of the protagonist from youth to adulthood. It is also known as the **novel of education** or the **novel of formation**, and is a type of the coming-of-age story. Coined by the philologist Karl Morgenstern in 1819, the German term '*Bildungsroman*' literally translates as 'formation novel'.

Features of a *Bildungsroman*

- The *Bildungsroman* narrates the story of the development of a sensitive person who goes in search of the meaning of life and of her/his place in society.

- A *Bildungsroman* generally begins with an emotional loss which compels the protagonist to set off on her/his journey.
- The protagonist faces several hurdles and failures along the way, and is often shown in conflict with the values of society.
- Eventually, and very gradually, the protagonist transforms from an inexperienced person to an emotionally mature individual.
- In the end, the protagonist accepts the values of society and is accepted into society.

This genre could be said to have evolved from folk tales in which a simple young man goes out into the world to seek his fortune. As a literary genre, the *Bildungsroman* came into being with the publication of Johann Wolfgang von Goethe's *Wilhelm Meister's Apprenticeship* (1795–96). This German novel had a great impact upon Europe and the rest of the world, and Goethe's translated work inspired several authors who began to write novels that traced the evolution of the protagonist. Examples of this genre are *Tom Jones* (1749) by Henry Fielding, *Jane Eyre* (1847) by Charlotte Brontë, *Great Expectations* (1861) by Charles Dickens, *The Catcher in the Rye* (1951) by J.D. Salinger, and *The Kite* Runner (2003) by Khaled Hosseini.

A variation of the *Bildungsroman* is the ***Künstlerroman*** (German for 'artist's novel') which traces the development of an artist or a writer. Charles Dickens's *David Copperfield* (1850) and James Joyce's *A Portrait of the Artist as a Young Man* (1916) are examples of this subgenre.

5

Literary Criticism

In the words of Lee T. Lemon, author and professor of English, literary criticism 'is a disciplined attempt to understand and to evaluate works of literature'. As it can achieve the above only through a close reading of texts, criticism is a result of a detailed examination of a literary work. The English critic Walter Pater defined criticism as 'the art of interpreting art'.

The word 'criticism' is derived from the Greek *κριτής* (*krités*) meaning 'judge', and that is the broadest sense in which it is used. A literary critic is therefore an expert who shares his knowledge and learning with the reader. Thus, as Thomas Carlyle says, 'criticism stands like an interpreter between the inspired and the uninspired; between the prophet and those who hear the melody of his words and catch some glimpse of their material meaning but understand not their deeper import'. The subtle nuances of an excellent piece of literature would remain unexplored without the critic's insightful remarks. Literature, in its various forms such as poetry, drama and fiction, is a reflection of life and the world we live in. Literary criticism interprets this reflection of life for us.

Functions of criticism

According to T.S. Eliot, 'criticism ... must always profess an end in view, which, roughly speaking, appears to be the elucidation of works of art and the correction of taste'. From this definition, we understand that the two functions of criticism are **interpretation** and **judgement**.

Criticism plays an important role in enhancing our appreciation of a literary text by interpreting the various subtle shades of meaning within it. The critic as interpreter acts as a pathfinder, helping the uninitiated reader gain a deeper understanding of the text. She/he analyses and penetrates into the heart of a book and helps to make explicit that which is implicit. In doing so, the critic is like a friendly companion who points out things that could go unnoticed. An example of such a critic is A.C. Bradley, as evidenced in his criticism of Shakespeare.

The other function of criticism, namely judgement, is an older concept and does not enjoy much favour now. Plato became the first 'judicial' critic when he banished poets from his ideal state. For centuries, judgement was seen as the sole function of criticism. The English academic Helen Gardner's metaphor of the sceptre and the torch, in her famous 1953 talk on criticism, aptly describes the twin functions of a critic—the sceptre symbolising judgement, and the torch, interpretation.

Although it is good for a reader to go to a secondary source in order to have a better understanding of an author or a text, she/he should not depend solely on the views of the critic. It is vital for a reader to have firsthand knowledge of the work in question. Criticism can never be used as a shortcut to knowledge as it is being done increasingly today. It can never take the place of literature and a reader should not satisfy herself/himself by merely reading what others have said about a work.

Qualities of an ideal critic

- A good critic should be knowledgeable. He should have read not only the book that he is critiquing, but should also have excellent knowledge about the genre, the age to which it belongs, and the background to its composition. He should be very familiar with the views and ideas of the author.
- A critic should be sensitive and perceptive.

- He should be unbiased and unprejudiced, and should approach the author and his work with an open mind. He should avoid all political and religious biases.
- A critic should be wary of succumbing to the temptation of exhibiting his own knowledge at the expense of sidelining the work that is being examined.
- A good critic should not engage in nitpicking. He should focus on what is good in the work.

Legislative Criticism

Legislative criticism is one of the earliest forms of criticism. The critic acts as a lawgiver. The ancient Greeks and Romans endeavoured to lay down rules for writers, who were expected to follow them without any questions. The works of these critics were based on the standard works of literature of their time. The Greeks Plato (circa 429–347BCE) and Aristotle (384–322BCE) were two of the earliest critics who attempted to systematically study works of art. Aristotle's *Poetics* is the first important critical treatise and it was written as early as the fourth century BCE. The writings of these critics were directed towards writers rather than readers. This type of criticism is archaic and is now seen only in books on composition or creative writing.

Pragmatic Criticism

This is another ancient form of criticism that can be traced back to the Roman poet–critic, Horace. The aim of pragmatic critics is to study the effect of a literary work on the audience (the receiver of the work). They believe that an author structures his work in such a way as to achieve a particular effect on the reader/audience. The pragmatic critic's job is to study and evaluate a work based on their observation of the success or failure of the work in achieving the desired effect. Horace (65–8BCE), in his *Ars Poetica* (*The Art of Poetry*, circa 19BCE), highlighted the effect of a literary work on its audience. This type of criticism was in vogue till the eighteenth century, after which it lost its popularity.

Judicial Criticism

This school of criticism is based firmly on the belief that a critic has to perform the role of a judge. Accordingly, the judicial critic attempts to analyse and elucidate a work of art by thoroughly dissecting it. He examines the work under several headings such as subject, style, organisation of ideas, and techniques. This method of criticism seeks to pronounce judgement on works of literature on the basis of certain rules. Only if the work is found to comply with the rules is it considered to be good. These rules were derived from the classical Greek and Roman critics like Aristotle and Horace.

This type of criticism was popular in the classical age. In the modern period, Samuel Johnson (1709–84) could be called a judicial critic, as he approached a poet and his works with the aim of passing verdict. His assessment of writers was not based on their individual merit, but upon their adherence to the classical rules of literary composition. His judgement, thus, was dogmatic and traditional.

Judicial criticism is frowned upon by modern scholars, as they feel that one cannot judge a contemporary work by standards set in a bygone age.

Biographical Criticism

This form of criticism analyses the biography of the writer and demonstrates the impact his life has had upon the work in question. This method dates back to the Renaissance period. One of its chief practitioners was Samuel Johnson, and his work *Lives of the Poets* (1779–81) is an example of biographical criticism.

This type of criticism has its advantages and disadvantages. If employed with discretion, the study of a writer's life can help us to appreciate some of the nuances of the work which we might otherwise have missed. At the same time, one should avoid making unnecessary connections and reading between the lines when there is nothing to be read. The biographical method must not be misused as a shortcut to understanding a text.

Biographical criticism remained popular throughout the nineteenth and twentieth centuries. It was attacked by the New Critics of the 1920s, who coined the term, 'biographical fallacy' to describe the process of interpreting a literary work based solely on biography.

Historical Criticism

This school of criticism is based on the hypothesis that true appreciation of a work is possible only when we place it against the background in which it was conceived. All works of art are seen as historical objects, written at a certain time in the past. Historical critics firmly believe that one cannot consider a work as an autonomous entity that can stand by itself. It can be truly appreciated only when the various factors that had influenced the author at the time of writing are taken into account and explained.

The chief aim of the historical critic is to determine the text's original meaning in its historical context. The time and place of the text's composition, its sources, and the important events, persons and customs depicted in it or associated with it are all thoroughly examined.

Comparative Criticism

This approach to the critical study of literature was popularised by the English poet and critic Matthew Arnold (1822–88). Arnold was a classicist in ideology and he upheld the works of the ancient Greek and Roman writers. He also admired certain English writers such as Spenser, Shakespeare and Milton. Arnold used certain select passages from them as touchstones to compare and judge the merit of contemporary literary works. This method of comparing modern works with ancient and classical works is known as the '**touchstone method**'.

The method has its limitations, as one cannot pick out random passages from texts, compare them, and arrive at a conclusion. A literary work has to be studied in its entirety. However, the comparative method is useful since it helps to set standards by which one can judge the merit of a work of art.

Inductive Criticism

Inductive criticism is based on the scientific investigation of a literary work. It believes that the laws of each author's work are to be discovered within the work itself. Hence, the laws of one work cannot be applied to another. In this, inductive criticism is diametrically opposite to judicial criticism, which bases its conclusions on the concept of literary standards.

This approach stresses the importance of scientific accuracy and impartiality. The inductive critic does not praise or blame a work, nor does he try to evaluate its merit. He merely reviews the work and does not indulge in sharing any personal opinions. The critic who is most commonly associated with inductive criticism is Richard Green Moulton (1849–1924), who extols its merits in the preface to his book, *Shakespeare as a Dramatic Artist* (1885).

Ecocriticism

Ecocriticism is the name given to the study literature from an ecological or environmental perspective. It is a study of the relationship between literature and the physical environment, between culture and nature. Just as feminist criticism examines language and literature from a gender-conscious perspective, and Marxist criticism brings an awareness of the modes of production and economic class to its reading of texts, ecocriticism takes an earth-centred approach to literary studies.

Other schools of criticism deal with the relations between writers, texts and the world. According to the ecocritics, the word 'world' includes the entire ecosphere, and not just human society. Literature is seen by them as part of a vastly complex global system. In this system, there is an interaction between matter, energy and ideas. Ecocritics focus upon issues such as how nature is represented in a poem, the role of the physical setting in the development of the plot of a novel, or the extent of ecological awareness in a play.

Ecocritics have sensitised readers into considering nature as an equally important critical category, along with considerations such as race, class and gender. They also raise questions about the role played by literature with regard to the global environmental crisis. Ecocritics try to draw our attention to the crisis towards which the modern world is racing. They firmly believe that literature can play a significant role in curbing it.

Some of the names associated with this school of thought are Ralph Waldo Emerson (1803–82), Margaret Fuller (1810–50), Henry David Thoreau (1817–62), and Mahasweta Devi (born 1926).

Psychoanalytic Criticism

Psychoanalytic criticism is a form of literary criticism which employs the techniques of **psychoanalysis** (exploring underlying motives in order to treat mental disorders) to interpret texts. It became popular in the 1920s. Its origin can be traced to the work of the Austrian psychoanalyst Sigmund Freud (1856–1939), who first used the term 'psychoanalysis' to describe his method of mental therapy. His book *The Interpretation of Dreams* (1900), which discusses his analytic interpretive process, became a model for this school of critics.

According to Freud and the psychoanalytic critics, the unconscious mind is a storehouse of desires, fears and inner conflicts. The unconscious is very powerful and plays an important role in shaping our personality and controlling our actions. Freud explained that the mind makes short visits to the unconscious when we dream. The events represented in dreams are compared to the events described in a literary text. Psychoanalytic critics interpret a literary text from this point of view in order to analyse the author or a particularly interesting character. Fictional characters are seen as case studies, and various Freudian concepts (such as the Oedipus complex, id, ego and super-ego) are identified in texts and their influence is studied. Freud himself has analysed some of Shakespeare's characters, most famously Hamlet, Macbeth and Lear.

The French psychoanalyst Jacques Lacan (1901–81) gave psychoanalysis a new twist by pointing out that the unconscious was rooted in language and, in turn, influenced it. He focused on language-related issues like symbols, metonymy and displacement.

Psychoanalytic criticism is very useful in unlocking perplexing symbols and actions in a literary work. However, one must guard against depending completely on a psychoanalytic reading of literature, as one may miss the wider significance of the work. Some of the best examples of this type of criticism are Marie Bonaparte's *Life and Works of Edgar Allan Poe: A Psycho-analytical Interpretation* (1933) and Ernest Jones's *Hamlet and Oedipus* (1949).

Sociological Criticism

This school of criticism focuses on the social environment to which the work belongs. The Russian political theorist Vladimir Lenin (1870–1924) believed that literature and society affected each other. Writers can be deeply influenced by the society they live in and by contemporary events; at the same time they can change society's way of thinking through their words. Sociological critics are of the opinion that an investigation of the relationship between the writer and society could greatly enrich one's understanding of a book. Since literature is rooted in society, it reflects the *zeitgeist* or the spirit of the age. As Wilbur Scott, professor of English, has put it, 'art is not created in a vacuum; it is the work not simply of a person, but of an author fixed in time and space, answering to a community of which he is an important member'. Sociological critics do not consider literature to be the expression of an individual mind, but rather a reflection of the entire society.

Hippolyte Taine (1828–93) was an important French sociological critic who taught scholars to approach literature scientifically. He is well-known for his formula of 'race, milieu and moment'. In this, 'race' stands for hereditary disposition; 'milieu' represents the writer's surroundings, which includes features such as climate, politics, topography and social conditions; and 'moment' refers to the immediate political or social development at the time of writing a work of literature. Taine strongly felt that it was vital for a reader to familiarise himself to all three of the above for a true and deep understanding of literature. Such an approach to literature is not without drawbacks. Taine makes it appear as if all the people living at a particular time are just samples of the age, without any individuality of their own. Another defect is that he ignores the effect that the author has upon the age. His attention is only upon how society has shaped an author.

Important sociological critics include Edmund Wilson (1895–1972), Kenneth Burke (1897–1993), Cecil Day-Lewis (1904–72), Stephen Spender (1909–95), and David Daiches (1912–2005).

Marxist Criticism

Marxist criticism is a special branch of sociological criticism which believes that the form and content of literature are closely related to historical, social and economic forces. This school of criticism is influenced by the theories of the German philosopher Karl Marx (1818–83).

Marx believed that all history was a struggle between the ruling class (or the capitalists) and the working class. This conflict impacted society which tried to device ingenious ways of preventing the exploited classes from rebelling. The methods to keep the downtrodden under check included laws, customs, traditions, religions and rituals. All these in turn had a deep influence on the personality, belief and action of the people. Marx urged the public to overcome this injustice by bringing about a revolution. Marx and his friend Friedrich Engels (1820–95) believed that the result of such a revolution would be the creation of a classless society.

Marx and Engels did not, however, develop any systematic aesthetic theory. Their ideas on literature and art were reflected in their philosophical, economic or political works and letters. Marx believed even literature to be just another social institution with a specific ideological function that was based on the background of the author. Marxist critics view literary works as reflections of the social institutions to which they belong, and analyse the class constructs demonstrated in them.

The ideas of Marx and Engels were developed by several other writers, the most notable of them being the Hungarian philosopher and critic Georg Lukács (1885–1971). Lukács had a lot of followers in Western Europe. The first British Marxist critic was Christopher Caudwell (1907–37), who studied Shakespeare, Milton, Wordsworth, Coleridge and other writers against the background of sociological and economic changes.

Marxist critics often disagreed among themselves. What is regarded as 'vulgar Marxism' sought to replace all canonical works of literature with works of **social realism**, an art movement which portrayed the lives of the poor and the oppressed. Critics such as Lukács were opposed to this, believing that nineteenth-century realist writers often captured social realities accurately in their works. However, Lukács was in turn opposed to modernist experiments, which he considered self-indulgent. The German Marxists Walter Benjamin (1892–1940), Bertolt Brecht (1898–1956), and Theodor Adorno (1903–69), on the other hand, praised modernist movements and non-realist modes of expression as being bold critiques of society. Marxist criticism has continued to evolve as a result of such dissension. Other important Marxist critics include Louis Althusser (1918–90), Fredric Jameson (born 1934) and Terry Eagleton (born 1943). Along with feminism and postcolonialism, Marxist criticism takes its place in history as a major twentieth-century mode of critical thought.

Russian Formalism

This school of criticism enjoyed its heydays in Russia from the 1910s to the 1930s.The chief scholars associated with this branch of criticism are Viktor Shklovsky (1893–1984), Yuri Tynyanov (1894–1943), Roman Jakobson (1896–1982) and Victor Erlich (1914–2007). They were critical of the biographical, historical, sociological and other extrinsic methods of studying a literary text. Instead, they focused on the functional role of literary devices and advocated a scientific method of analysing language.

The Russian formalists did not have any unified doctrine; however, they were united in agreeing on the autonomous nature of poetic language. They believed that the features of literature are unique and that it is distinct from other human activities. It therefore requires a specialised method of study focusing only on the analysis of its form, instead of emphasising philosophical, psychological, historical or other issues. They firmly believed that art was a matter of style and technique, and so they concentrated on formal patterns and technical devices, rather than on the subject of a work or the values it espouses. Russian formalism was a major influence on structuralism and the poststructuralism.

New Criticism

This refers to a school of literary criticism that became popular in America and England from the 1920s. The term 'New Criticism' was applied to the new wave in critical thought after the American scholar John Crowe Ransom (1888–1974) published a book entitled *The New Criticism* in 1941.

The New Critics believed that the meaning of a work of literature was inseparable from its structure. They, therefore, strongly advocated a close reading of texts. A literary piece was examined as a linguistic structure in which all the parts are held together by tension, paradox, irony or ambiguity. They focused on elements such as plot, metre, symbols, images, and so on. The New Critics rejected the historical, biographical, and comparative approaches, as they felt that these methods erroneously look at factors that are external to a text. They also pointed out that an author's intended meaning or aim is irrelevant to literary analysis; the only meaning that mattered was that which the text itself provided. Similarly, a work cannot be judged based on a reader's response to it, as that, too, is extraneous to the text.

New Criticism shared many common features with Russian formalism. Both kinds of criticism focused on exploring the specifically literary aspects of a text. Both also vehemently rejected the subjective and spiritual interpretation that the Romantics gave to reading. They differed only in their approach. The formalists believed that form was more important than content; to them, content was merely the means to create organised, literary forms. However, to the New Critics, form and content were inseparable. As a result of their differing principles, the formalists tended to focus on genres and general literary devices, while the New Critics preferred to examine individual texts.

Some of the important critics who belonged to this group were Allen Tate (1899–1979), R.P. Blackmur (1904–65), Robert Penn Warren (1905–89), Cleanth Brooks (1906–94), W.K. Wimsatt (1907–75), and Monroe Beardsley (1915–85). New Criticism had a very big impact upon critical attitudes and played an important role in doing away with amateurish studies of literature that were based on historical and biographical approaches.

Feminist Criticism

Feminist criticism is a re-examination of the misrepresentation of women in literature down the ages. It is the contention of feminist critics that women have been constantly marginalised and treated as the 'other' in a male-dominated world. They look at how our culture is essentially patriarchal and try to expose the misogynistic representation of women in male writing about women. Feminist criticism also concerns itself with issues such as the exclusion of women writers from the traditional literary cannon, the prejudice of male critics and publishers, and women's economic condition as authors. The goal of these critics is to bring about a global change in the attitude towards women and to establish equality of the sexes.

Feminist criticism can be looked at from two angles—women as readers and women as writers. The first category is a revisiting of popular and classical literary works from a feminist point of view and re-evaluating them. The second tries to foreground forgotten or neglected women writers of the past and to compile a body of literature by and about women.

Some of the important thinkers who revolutionised literary criticism into including space for women and their writings are Virginia Woolf (*A Room of One's Own*, 1929), Simone de Beauvoir (*The Second Sex*, 1949), Mary Ellmann (*Thinking about Women*, 1968) and Elaine Showalter (*A Literature of their Own*, 1977).

Archetypal Criticism

Archetype means a basic prototype or original pattern from which copies are made. It is derived from the Greek words *ἀρχή* (*archē*), which means 'beginning', and *τύπος* (*tupos*), which means 'imprint'. Archetypal criticism is a branch of literary criticism that interprets a literary text by focusing on the recurring myths and patterns in the narrative, imagery, characters and symbols. These critics made extensive use of James Frazer's *The Golden Bough* (1890), which is a comprehensive guide to the myths, rituals and primitive religious practices of different societies of the world.

The Swiss psychotherapist Carl Jung's contribution to the development of archetypal criticism is significant for it was he who pointed out the presence of what he referred to as the 'collective unconscious'. He theorised that the experiences of all our ancestors gets collected and is stored in some unconscious recess of the human mind. Therefore, when we create, we unconsciously go back to these archetypes. All human lives go through archetypal functions like birth, death, conflict, love and other issues which can be grouped into fixed patterns. Similarly, certain character or personality types too are archetypal. For example, the hero, the rebel, the Don Juan (the philanderer), the snob, the damsel in distress, the wicked stepmother, etc., are all archetypal figures.

An archetypal critic devotes himself to detecting archetypal figures and patterns in literature. The origin of this school of criticism can be traced to Maud Bodkin's *Archetypal Patterns in Poetry* published in 1934. It reached the pinnacle of its popularity in the 1940s and 1950s. The Canadian critic Northrop Frye (1912–91) is one of the most prominent figures of this school of criticism.

Structuralist Criticism

Structuralist criticism, which appeared in the 1960s, is a study of language that focuses not on the communicative function of language, but on examining the conditions that allow language and meaning to arise. Structuralist criticism questions how the elements of language are organised in order to yield the effect it has.

The principles of structuralism can be traced to work of the Swiss linguist Ferdinand de Saussure (1857–1913), who pointed out that language was not a random collection of words, but one that contained a structured system of relationships. Saussure showed that a word was a linguistic sign and has two interrelated sides to it—the **signifier** and the **signified**. The signifier refers to the sound image or the word (for example, the word 'dog'); the signified is the concept which is being referred to by the signifier (that is, the actual dog itself). The relationship between the signifier and the signified is very arbitrary (the letters that form the written word 'dog' or the sounds that constitute the spoken word 'dog' have no real connection to the living animal they represent), but they work together to create meaning. But the meaning of a signifier can only be understood in relation to other signifiers (we know what 'spoon' signifies, because we can differentiate it from a 'fork' or a 'knife'). Signs are often understood in terms of **binary opposites** such as light–dark, strong–weak, realist–romantic, and capitalist–socialist. Thus we see that there exists a vast and complex system of interrelated signs which derive their meaning based on their differences from and relation to one another. Language consists of artificial constructs—a system of structures—that mediates between us and external reality.

Discovering the system of structures that create meaning in literature was the main focus of the structuralist school of criticism. Structuralist critics try to examine how these artificial constructs work. They do not try to interpret the meaning of an individual work or judge it. They are more interested in language and grammar, and focus on the narrative structures. They preferred the word 'text' to 'work', to emphasise their point that all literature was subject to a set of codes rather than being a unique product of the author's mind. They also questioned the belief that the text was a representation of reality, as they believed that all signification was arbitrary.

The most important figures connected with this school of thought are Claude Lévi-Strauss (1908–2009), Lucien Goldmann (1913–70), Roland Barthes (1915–80), Louis Althusser (1918–90), and Jonathan Culler (born 1944).

Poststructuralist Criticism

Poststructuralism, which arose in the late 1960s, could be understood as a blanket term used to represent those radical theories which opposed structuralism. Structuralism posits that there is a structure of meaning below the surface level of signs; poststructuralists reject the possibility of any single determinate meaning.

Influenced by the concept of **deconstruction** (exposing deep-seated contradictions in a work by delving below its surface meaning), poststructuralism tried to formulate new theories concerning interpretation and meaning. The notion of deconstruction was based on three books *Speech and Phenomena*, *Of Grammatology*, and *Writing and Difference* (all three first published in 1967) by the French philosopher Jacques Derrida (1930–2004).

According to Derrida, all notions of the existence of an absolute meaning in language are incorrect. Both the author and the reader of a text are influenced by unconscious biases. These inherent biases affect the examination of the underlying structure of any cultural product. Besides, signifiers often do not point to a signified, but to other signifiers. Even binary oppositions cannot yield fixed meanings, only relative ones: since both terms are dependent on the other for meaning, neither term can claim greater significance or establish a single point of reference or meaning. We can only 'de-construct' artificial constructs and analyse how various factors contribute to multiple meanings and the contradictory nature of texts.

Thus, while structuralism looks upon structures and patterns as providing the key to meaning, poststructuralism looks upon all structures with deep mistrust and declares the quest for a fixed meaning as illusory and misleading. Apart from Derrida, other poststructuralist critics include Jacques Lacan (1901–81), Gilles Deleuze (1925–95), Michel Foucault (1926–84), Jean Baudrillard (1929–2007), and Judith Butler (born 1956).

Reader-response Criticism

This school of criticism focuses on the reader and his response to a work of literature rather than on the author or on the work itself. It sees the reader as an active agent who completes the work of the author by making it come alive through his own interpretation. It is in complete opposition to the tenets of formalism and New Criticism, which ignore the psychology of the reader and the reader's role in recreating a text.

Reader-response critics examine the numerous responses of various readers to a given work and try to see if the responses are similar to the meaning(s). They also try to observe if a work can have as many meanings as there are responses and if some responses are more valid than others. Reader-response critics do not see the reader as a passive recipient of a literary work but as an active co-creator of the work.

This school of criticism became popular in the United States in the 1970s, although its attitudes can be traced in several critics long before that. For example, the English critic I.A. Richards (1893–1979), in his *Practical Criticism* (1929), argued that readers' feelings and experiences acted as a way of authenticating the representation of emotions and events in a literary text.

The origin of reader-response criticism could be traced to the American theorist Stanley Fish (born 1938), who argued that any school of criticism that looks at a work of literature as an artefact to simply be analysed is doing gross injustice to the work. He attacked the formalists for looking at a work as a mere object and not taking into consideration that it might appear differently to different readers. The German critic Wolfgang Iser (1926–2007) pointed out that there are gaps in a text that have a great impact upon the reader. The reader is forced to make the necessary connections and create for himself what is not directly seen in the text, but what is implicitly implied by the author. The reader thus becomes an active meaning-maker. Another important critic of this school was Louise M. Rosenblatt (1904–2005).

Phenomenological criticism

The word 'phenomenology' is derived from the Greek terms *φαινόμενον* ('*phainómenon*') meaning 'that which appears' and *λόγος* ('lógos') meaning 'study'. The German philosopher Edmund Husserl (1859–1938) is considered to be the founder of this school of thought. He believed that experience was the source of all knowledge. The chief aim of this school of thought was to directly investigate and describe the structures of experience and consciousness, without tying them down to any theories or trying to discover a cause.

The term 'phenomenology' is much older and can be traced to the works of earlier philosophers. The German philosopher Georg Friedrich Hegel (1770–1831) was preoccupied with this concept. In his book *Phenomenology of Mind* (1807), Hegel traced the journey of the human spirit from mere experience to complete knowledge. He used the term to describe the study of the appearance of consciousness.

The Geneva School of critics—a group of critics associated with the University of Geneva in the 1950s and 1960s—used the phenomenological method in their analysis of works of literature. Some of the prominent names associated with this school were the Belgian Georges Poulet (1902–91), the French Jean-Pierre Richard (born 1922), the Swiss critics Marcel Raymond (1897–1981), Albert Béguin (1901–57) and Jean Rousset (1910–2002). They examined literature as being representations of the deep structures of an author's consciousness and his or her relationship with the world outside. They were not concerned with biographical criticism and instead focused primarily on the work itself. They studied such aspects of a literary work as the recurrent themes and images and the communication between the self and the others.

Postcolonial Criticism

Postcolonial criticism is concerned with the literature produced by the coloniser and the colonised. Postcolonial theory examines issues such as politics, religion and culture, and how they were eclipsed by colonial **hegemony** (the domination of one social group or nation over others).

Postcolonial critics look at classics such as Daniel Defoe's *Robinson Crusoe* from a postcolonial perspective. In a postcolonial interpretation, Crusoe's gradual possession of the island and his condescending attitude toward the native man (whom he calls 'Friday') are foregrounded. Similarly, in a postcolonial interpretation of Shakespeare's *The Tempest*, Prospero's relationship with Caliban is severely criticised. Caliban, one of the antagonists of the play, is seen as a typical symbol of exploited peoples everywhere—treated as a slave in his own land.

Postcolonial criticism is also interested in questioning the western literary canon and the western version of history. Terms such as 'First World', 'Second World', 'Third World' and 'Fourth World' are rejected and critiqued by postcolonial critics. Since all history has been written by the so-called First World nations, historical narratives are seen as being highly prejudiced. They also question the exclusion of works by non-western writers from the so-called canon of literature (the body of art that is regarded as the most important in culture).

The Palestinian American intellectual Edward Said's *Orientalism* (1978) is seen as the pioneering work of postcolonial criticism. In it, he pointed out how the First World painted false images and myths about the Third World in order to justify their exploitation and domination over those countries. Another example of postcolonial criticism is the essay 'Postcolonial Criticism' (1992) by Homi K.Bhabha. He, too, points out how certain cultures expand their domination by misrepresenting other cultures. Other influential postcolonial critics include Frantz Fanon (1925–61) and Gayatri Chakravorty Spivak (born 1942).

Cognitive Criticism

This school of criticism makes use of the principles of **cognitive psychology** (the study of mental processes concerned with activities that involve language usage such as memory, problem-solving and creativity). Cognitive criticism is closely related to reader-response criticism and **stylistics** (the study of texts based on their linguistic style; it links literary criticism to linguistics). Critics practising this method of criticism engage in a close reading of the text and try to highlight the importance of context in the creation of meaning.

Cognitive criticism emerged in the 1980s, when critics took reader-response theory a step further. They argued that questions of literary interpretation are not dependent on just the reader, but that they are firmly rooted in their bodies and minds. By expanding the range of tools available for literary analysis, cognitive critics hope to open up new pathways for literary criticism and critical theory. The focus is on how readers process the language.

One of the primary concerns of this school of criticism is the idea of conceptual metaphor, which was explored by George Lakoff and Mark Johnson in their work *Metaphors We Live By* (1980). Conceptual metaphors refer to the understanding of one idea in terms of another. For example, the metaphor 'life is a journey' shapes our language in such a way as to make us view life as a journey that has to be undertaken, one in which we meet several co-travellers, etc. According to Lakoff and Johnson, metaphors are not mere decorative figures of speech, but important aspects of language that help us in understanding how the conceptual origins of such metaphors are interrelated to the text as a whole.

Critics who are associated with this school include Reuven Tsur (born 1932), Ronald Langacker (born 1942), and Mark Turner (born 1954)—all eminent linguists.

New Historicism

This school of criticism, influenced by structuralist and poststructuralist theories, aims at reconnecting a work with the age or time period in which it was produced. It attempts to interpret a work by identifying it with the political and cultural movements of the age to which it belongs. The assumption of the New Historicists is that every work is a product of the historic moment in which it was created.

The approach of the New Historicist is different from that of the traditional historian. The traditional historian is interested in a linear representation of history as a series of events based on the principle of cause and effect. The New Historicist, on the other hand, is more interested in studying how a particular event in history has been interpreted, and in examining how the interpretation reflects the sociopolitical leanings of the interpreter. According to the New Historicists, history can never be objective, as it depends on the person who is recording an event.

A New Historicist therefore studies a text against the background of the historical age to which it belongs. Equal importance is given to literary and non-literary texts, and both are studied together. The American critic Stephen Greenblatt (born 1943) popularised New Historicism.

References

Carlyle, Thomas. *Critical and Miscellaneous Essays: Collected & Republished in Five Volumes.* London: James Fraser, 1840.

Carlyle, Thomas. *The Hero as Poet*. Whitefish, Montana: Kessinger Publishing, 2010.

Eliot, T.S. *Selected Essays 1917–1932.* USA: Harcourt, Brace & Co, 1932.

Esslin, Martin. *The Theatre of the Absurd*. UK: Vintage, 2004.

Hudson, William Henry. *An Introduction to the Study of English Literature.* London: George G. Harrap & Co. Ltd., 1965.

Ionesco, Eugene. *The Chairs*. London: Faber and Faber, 2007.

Johnson, Samuel. *The Samuel Johnson Encyclopedia*. Westport: Greenwood Press, 1996.

Lemon, Lee T. *A Glossary for the Study of English*. Oxford University Press, 1971.

Saintsbury, George. *A Short History of English Literature.* London: Macmillan, 1912.

Scott, Wilbur S. *Five Approaches of Literary Criticism*. London: Collier-Macmillan Publishers, 1977.

Acknowledgements

All images sourced from Wikimedia Commons.

Image A (Page 7): 'The tragical ballad: or, the lady who fell in love with her serving-man' (Source: Eighteenth Century Collections Online).

Image B (Page 44): 'Amphitheater in Epidaurus' (7 June 2007) by Fingalo, used under a Creative Commons Attribution-ShareAlike 2.0 Germany license (http://creativecommons.org/licenses/by-sa/2.0/de/deed.en). Desaturated from original.

Image C (Page 54): Conjectural reconstruction of the Globe theatre by C. Walter Hodges, 1958 (Source: Folger Shakespeare Library http://goo.gl/5S1gIz), used under a Creative Commons Attribution-ShareAlike 4.0 International license (http://creativecommons.org/licenses/by-sa/4.0/deed.en). Cropped from original.

Image D (Page 56): C. Walter Hodges' imagined reconstruction of Shakespeare's Merchant of Venice, act 1, scene 3, being performed in an Elizabethan theatre. Drawn for *The Globe Restored*, published by Ernest Benn, 1953. (source: Folger Shakespeare Library http://luna.folger.edu/luna/servlet/s/5b1ps6), used under a Creative Commons Attribution-ShareAlike 4.0 International license (http://creativecommons.org/licenses/by-sa/4.0/deed.en). Desaturated from original.

Image E (Page 79): Fordham Theatre, Fordham Road and Valentine Avenue, Bronx, New York. William. H. McElfatrick, architect. Unknown photographer. (Source: *Architecture and Building*. Vol. 53 No. 5 (May 1921) Plate 75.

IMAGE F (PAGE 80): 'Cockpit Theatre (Marylebone), Auditorium view from upstage-left' by Onthemat (September 2006). Cockpit Theatre, Gateforth Street, London NW8 8EH, UK. Used under a Creative Commons Attribution-ShareAlike 3.0license (http://creativecommons.org/licenses/by-sa/3.0/). Desaturated from original.

IMAGE G (PAGE 81): Pasant Theatre thrust stage from seats (10 January 2007). Wharton Center. Used under a Creative Commons Attribution-Share Alike 3.0 Unported license (http://creativecommons.org/licenses/by-sa/3.0/deed.en). Desaturated from original.

